MASTERING
WORSHIP

MASTERING
WORSHIP

Jack Hayford
John Killinger
Howard Stevenson

MULTNOMAH

Portland, Oregon 97266

Christianity Today, Inc.

MASTERING WORSHIP
© 1990 by Christianity Today, Inc.
Published by Multnomah Press
Portland, Oregon 97266

Multnomah Press is a ministry of Multnomah School of the Bible, 8435 N.E. Glisan Street, Portland, Oregon 97220.

Printed in the United States of America.

Library of Congress Cataloging-in-Publication Data

Hayford, Jack W.
    Mastering worship / Jack Hayford, John Killinger, Howard Stevenson.
        p.   cm.
    ISBN 0-88070-364-4
    1. Public worship. I. Killinger, John. II. Stevenson, Howard. III. Title.
BV20.H39 1990
264—dc20   90-44164
                                                                CIP

90 91 92 93 94 95 96 97 98 99 - 10 9 8 7 6 5 4 3 2 1

CONTENTS

Introduction

It was just a pile of wood — ordinary, run-of-the-mill, common-as-sawdust wood. And a lay person standing near it, but not too near, was just praying, and not very professionally. But suddenly the place exploded in flames. Everyone, including the prominent clergy, fell on their knees in fear and awe, overwhelmed by the power and glory of the God.

The story of Elijah and the prophets of Baal reminds us of a truth most worshipers of the Lord God have discovered: worship can be explosive.

The early Jerusalem Christians discovered it when they

prayed and "the place where they were meeting was shaken. And they were all filled with the Holy Spirit and spoke the word of God boldly."

The church at Corinth discovered it, and they couldn't control themselves. The American colonies discovered it and called it the Great Awakening.

Most pastors have discovered it and go into ministry to lead others to discover the power of an encounter with God. But worship leaders often become frustrated, because sometimes the only great awakening they witness is that which happens when the service ends.

Of course, pastors cannot invoke the dynamite of God by reciting right liturgy or praying with passion. Modern prophets of Baal will be as disappointed as those ancient clergy when they couldn't call down fire at will. In that sense, no one can master worship, for worship is a process whereby we become mastered by Another.

On the other hand, pastors have been entrusted with the sacred responsibility of leading people in the worship of almighty God. And they are not satisfied if things simply run smoothly. They may heed Paul's advice, that everything be done decently and in order, but they also want their people to experience something of the Corinthian enthusiasm and to feel Elijah's fire.

Although pastors cannot direct God any more than they can manage a gale, they can lead worship so that the service doesn't deflect the winds of the Spirit, so that people are ready and able to hear his coming and be swept up in worship and praise.

How pastors prepare themselves and the service, how singing is led and special music presented, how prayers are articulated, how emotions are engaged, how creativity is encouraged, how visitors are included — how pastors carry out these mundane, common-as-sawdust responsibilities can make a difference in the degree and intensity of the fire come from on high.

Three worship leaders whose churches are known for and meaningful worship have joined together in this volume of *Mastering Ministry* to share their insights and experience in leading worship. They make no claim to have mastered worship, but they are recognized as models of the ongoing process of mastering skills necessary to lead people effectively in the praise of God.

John Killinger

In John Killinger's study in his in Lynchburg, Virginia, church hung a picture of a pastor, his hands folded in prayer and his chin pulled, turtle-like, into a clerical collar that covered his mouth.

In one sense, one would not think that a representation of John Killinger, a man from whom words — melodic, well-formed and articulated, intelligent words — flow like crystal water from a spring, words that delight, words that speak for worshipers their inmost longings, words that echo the Psalms, words that usher worshipers into the presence of God.

Yet, John also knows the value of silence. He is a worship leader awed by the task and fully aware of the power of words for good and bad. He almost expects his lips, like Isaiah's, to be seared, lest he speak as Peter did on the Mount of Transfiguration — saying anything just to fill the dead space of awesome silence.

"I'm painfully aware of the distance between my spiritual life and where I ought to be as someone who dares say anything about God," he once said in an interview with LEADERSHIP. "We preachers can talk so much about holy things that we dull our own sense of the richness.

"I once wrote Sister Corita Kent, who made such beautiful posters, asking her to lead worship services at Vanderbilt. I received a postcard from her. All it said was, 'Dear, I'm trying to be quiet.' It has haunted me for years.

"Just the fact that you're put on a pedestal as people's spiritual example is one of the most damnable things that can happen to you. You are subject to the danger of having something to say on every occasion — and saying it. After a while, you're lulled by the sound of your own voice, by the fact that other people seem to think you know what you're talking about.

"One of the dangers in ministry is that we talk on every occasion, often concerning things we ought to be quiet about. We all need time to be in the presence of God with the kind of intensity that changes the very texture of our souls."

John wants his worshipful words to count and his silences to prepare him to speak the words for and with the people in worship.

John first pastored at 18 in a little church in Kentucky, the state in which he eventually received a Ph.D. in English from the University of Kentucky. A Th.D. in homiletics and liturgics from Princeton Theological Seminary followed, as did an S.T.B. from Harvard.

Throughout his vocational pilgrimage, he has combined the academic and the practical. He pastored churches during many of his years as student and instructor. Then he spent fifteen years at Vanderbilt Divinity School as professor of preaching. Near midlife, he began feeling a touch removed from practical ministry, even though it was his academic field. So he took a pastorate at First Presbyterian Church in Lynchburg, Virginia, and then at First Congregational Church on bustling Wilshire Boulevard in Los Angeles.

In 1989 he returned to an academic setting as distinguished professor of religion and culture at Samford University in Birmingham, Alabama.

John's other books include *To My People with Love: The Ten Commandments for Today, The Tender Shepherd, Christ and the Seasons of Marriage, Christmas Spoken Here,* and *Fundamentals of Preaching.*

Howard Stevenson

Howard Stevenson leads worship for seven thousand people each Sunday at First Evangelical Free Church of Fullerton, California, although he lets some other fellow do the preaching.

Howard does such a good job that the other fellow, Charles Swindoll, doesn't allow his sermon time to eat into the worship period.

"Some people think that in a church like ours," says Howard, "with a nationally recognized communicator in the pulpit, worship means only a couple of stanzas of a hymn and then getting out of the way to turn Chuck loose. But we spend twenty-five to thirty minutes in worship prior to the sermon. I'm sure some people consider this as mere warm-up to the main event. But those people don't understand the heart of Chuck Swindoll. As Chuck has made clear many times, great preaching emerges out of great worship. When people have experienced the wonder and awe and majesty of worship, they're prepared to hear God's Word. They discover the gospel involves both emotion and information."

Helping people know the emotion of the gospel is Howard's job. And he helps them know it through his creative use of music and readings, as well as an impressive attention to detail and an ability to work well with others.

"Whatever the leadership style," he says "teamwork is vital to worshiping well. Every Sunday morning before worship begins, I write our organist, Margaret, a note. It might be something like, 'The choir and instrumentalists will begin "Great Is the Lord." But it might be good for you to do your prelude to worship in the key of C.' I don't want her playing the prelude in G-flat or something, and then make the trumpets, who begin the next piece, all of a sudden have to establish a new key.

"I also send a note to Chuck concerning, for example, what happens right after a song. 'Chuck, if you could pray along this line, if it's natural, in your own words. . . .' " In that way, a song doesn't have to end but can continue into prayer and make for a beautiful moment.

The result of such passion for worship and attention to detail? A service that doesn't distract people from worship, but engages their hearts and minds and focuses them on God.

Howard's interest in music began at age 8 with violin lessons. He was nurtured musically and spiritually at Mount Hermon Conference Grounds in California. He attended Westmont College in Santa Barbara and earned a M.A. in conducting from the University of Washington and a doctorate (D.M.A.) in choral and church music from the University of Southern California.

He has traveled extensively, using his musical leadership skills at dozens of conferences, and taught music at high schools and colleges, his last stint of seventeen years being at Westmont

College. He's been minister of music at First Evangelical Free
Church in Fullerton since 1980.

Jack Hayford

Jack Hayford believes in *leading* worship. "Some people suggest that a person who leads assertively in worship manipulates
people," he says. "Well, no one wants to be guilty of manipulation,
so some worship leaders hesitate to appear too directive.

"For example, I was asked to lead worship at one session of
the Lausanne Congress in Manila. I taught a simple chorus with a
tender melody and words that say, 'Holy Spirit come. / Make my
ears to hear, / My eyes to see, / My mouth to speak, / My heart to
seek, / And my hand to reach out and touch the world with your
love.'

"I introduced the song by saying, 'I've found as I sing this
song that it helps me to touch the parts of my body as the song refers
to them,' and I invited people to do so. This generally was well
received, but, as will happen any time you try something new, a few
people were uncomfortable. One of the leaders said I had manipulated the crowd.

"The next night, however, this leader led the conference
through the Lord's Supper. He used an Anglican liturgy, which I
enjoyed. At his bidding we read together from printed sheets. Then
he instructed us in how to partake of the Supper.

"I suppose I could have criticized him for manipulating us.
But that would have been a pile of bosh. He was no more manipula-
tive than I was. Each of us was simply leading. That's what we're
called to do: lead worship so that people can praise God with freedom and joy. We just had two different ways of doing it."

Jack has been leading people in worship for more than thirty-
eight years. After graduating from LIFE Bible College in Los Angeles, he took a pastorate in Fort Wayne, Indiana. He returned to
Los Angeles to serve as National Youth Director for the Interna-
tional Church of the Foursquare Gospel and then became a professor at LIFE. In 1969 he began a "temporary assignment" to pastor
eighteen people at Church on the Way in Van Nuys, California.

Today nearly ten thousand attend weekly services, and Jack continues to pastor. He has written several books, including *Worship His Majesty* and *Rebuilding the Real You*. He is also writes songs, and perhaps his best known composition is the hymn "Majesty."

Prepare for Worship!

Annie Dillard in her essay "Expedition to the North Pole" reflects on Christian worship and asks, "Does anyone have the foggiest idea what sort of power we so blithely invoke? The churches are children playing on the floor with their chemistry sets, mixing up a batch of TNT to kill a Sunday morning. It is madness to wear ladies' straw hats and velvet hats to church; we should all be wearing crash helmets. Ushers should issue life preservers and signal flares: they should lash us to our pews."

It would be too much to promise that, after reading this book, your worship services will explode with spiritual vibrancy. As these authors are the first to admit, we can't manipulate the Almighty.

Yet we're sure these authors will allow you to see new possibilities for congregational praise and fresh ways to help people open themselves to the Spirit in worship. And if that happens, you may just find yourself adding a couple of items to your ushers' list of duties.

— Mark Galli
associate editor
LEADERSHIP Journal
Carol Stream, Illinois

PART ONE

Preparation

Prayer sensitizes us to the true meaning of worship. The person who spends time within the divine circle of companionship never enters the hour of worship without being sensitive to what can occur there.

— John Killinger

The Intangible Side of Worship

Several years ago I was preaching in a small Tennessee church. From the minute I entered the sanctuary, I felt a spirit there I hadn't felt in many sanctuaries. The prayers, the music, and even the silences were extraordinary. I feel sure that I preached over my head — that my own spirit was measurably quickened and deepened by the unusual sense of worship prevailing in the minister and the congregation.

Later, I commented about this to two laymen.

"I hope you know," I said, "what a rare and exhilarating kind of worship you enjoy in this church."

They smiled knowingly at one another. "Have you seen The Cloisters?" one asked. I wasn't sure what they were referring to — surely not the assemblage of monastery remains brought to New York by John D. Rockefeller, Jr.

"The shed up in the woods behind the preacher's house," one of them added when he saw my perplexity.

I had seen the building, but I didn't know it by the name they used.

"That's what the preacher calls it," they said. "It's where he goes to pray. And sometimes he takes some of us there, too. He goes up there every Saturday evening to pray for our services on Sunday. His wife says sometimes he stays two or three hours."

The mystery of the great worship services suddenly evaporated.

It was not a large congregation. They had no dynamic, colorful song leader. None of the cues were evident that usually indicate an exciting, impressive service of worship. But the most important ingredient of all was present: the minister and his people were prepared spiritually to come before God.

Catered Worship

Unfortunately, too much worship is constructed and performed with little such spiritual preparation.

How easily I can begin to process worship like a caterer who's served a thousand meals and now can do it blindfolded, who knows precisely how many gallons of anchovies and olives he needs for the salad trays and how many mousses and strawberry parfaits for the desserts. I can begin to approach worship with the nonchalance and casualness born of years in the ministry, no longer stopping to wonder if what I'm doing is pleasing to God, or if God is going to work mightily in the souls of the people as they worship.

Isn't that true for any of us? We begin to concern ourselves principally with whether the service will be well attended ("Had a great service today — chairs in the aisles!") and if it will proceed without snags or glitches ("It went beautifully this morning, without a bobble!").

As we well know but sometimes forget, our greater care ought to be about how *God* regards our worship. It matters not how many attend or how glitch-free our performance is if, when we are done, the Almighty says, as he did in the days of Amos, "Come to Bethel (or church), and transgress; to Gilgal (or church), and multiply transgression . . . for so you love to do, O people of Israel!" (Amos 4:4–5).

Many church attenders don't necessarily miss the spiritual dimension. They tend to leave that sort of thing to "the experts." But they do know if they're getting anything out of the time they spend in the sanctuary.

Suppose they finally make the connection between their boredom and the absence of God. That's a sobering thought, isn't it? It would mean they know I've failed in my role as a spiritual leader, that I'm fulfilling only the technical side of my responsibilities, that I'm not measuring up on the truly important matters.

Our Job First

Worship preparation *is* basically my responsibility as pastor. Oh, congregations are responsible too. They make an enormous difference with their prayers and enthusiasm and healthy participation. But they aren't the leaders and can hardly be expected to provide the thrust toward more spiritual services. According to biblical warrant, that is *my* venue — and yours.

If we don't prepare spiritually for worship, it's highly unlikely that the Spirit will be felt in the service, or that the individual parts of the liturgy will rise and converge into an exciting whole.

Let's admit we are busy people — pastoral CEOS — and we're prone to try to "work up" the sense of worship from our side, without pausing to think what we are doing when we gather to invoke the presence of the Great Mystery. A tribe of African fishermen, I've been told, padded the oars of their canoes when they entered certain lakes. Impressed by the sacredness of their environs, they took care to muffle their strokes. What happens when *we* feel that way about approaching the Almighty in worship? It transforms our understanding of how worship occurs. We see technique as much less important than an awareness of God's presence.

Sensitized to Worship

What helps sensitize us to true worship?

Certainly prayer. The person who spends time within the circle of divine companionship becomes acutely aware of the way all of life is transmuted by that experience and never enters the hour of worship without being sensitive to what can occur there. Like writer John Updike, who says he never can pass a bookstore without thinking, *There's a book in there that can change my life,* the prayerful worshiper knows that he or she stands at the threshold of a potentially new and radically different existence.

Music is another avenue — especially the great choral and instrumental music of our faith. For a long time it has been the habit in our household, early on Sunday morning when I am grooming to leave for church, for my wife to sit at the piano and evoke the marvelously compelling melodies of our religious past — the choruses that charmed us, the beautiful hymns that helped to set our theology, the glorious anthems that transported us. Whatever my mood when she begins, the music overpowers me, and I'm caught up in a spirit of excitement and enthusiasm for worship.

I thoroughly approve of the practice I have found in some churches to have a hymn- or chorus-sing for twenty or thirty minutes prior to the appointed time for the service. It warms people's souls for worship as few things can.

Apt words sometimes help remind us of the true enchantment of worshiping God. We may prepare ourselves by spending a few minutes with a book by Carlo Caretto or another great devotionalist. We can help the congregation by reading aloud a few prefatory statements about worship, or by printing them on the worship bulletin.

Here is a "poem" I found framed at the entrance to the village church in Hawkshead, England, where William Wordsworth worshiped as a schoolboy:

No man entering a house
ignores him who dwells there

> This is the house of God
> and he is here
>
> Pray then to him who loves you
> and bids you welcome
>
> Give thanks
> for those who in years past
> built this place to his glory
>
> Rejoice
> in his gifts of beauty
> in art and music
> architecture and handicrafts
>
> And worship him
> the one God Father of us all
> through our Lord and Savior
> Jesus Christ.
>
> Amen.

I've used this in my own worship bulletin to inspire my people to know what they do when they worship.

It comes down to *our* sense of expectancy as we approach worship, and how we can create similar expectancy in our congregations. Perhaps a simple ritual, such as removing our shoes for a moment before entering the sanctuary on Sunday morning, would maintain a proper sense in ourselves. But what else can we do for our people?

A Heritage of Worship

I've found study of the history and theology of worship provides an enormous thrust to most people's sense of what is occurring — or supposed to occur — when they worship. It deepens their understanding and sharpens their feeling of participation, and hence creates a greater mood of excitement and mystery.

When I was pastor of the First Presbyterian Church of Lynchburg, Virginia, I talked with the worship committee about conducting a course of study for them. They were pleased with the idea but suggested that if it was good for them, it also would be good for others. So we opened the course to the congregation and were surprised when nearly one hundred persons signed up for a ten-week Sunday-evening series on the history and meaning of worship.

We began with a study of Jewish worship as it existed in the time of Jesus, and showed how, with the addition of the Lord's Supper, it became the basis for early Christian worship. Then we saw how the legalization of worship and the building of Christian sanctuaries led to more involved and formalized liturgies, eventually issuing in the complicated form of the Mass in the later Middle Ages. Naturally, excitement rose about the revision of worship under the sixteenth-century Reformers, and subsequent developments as the various liturgical traditions encountered the American frontier. (Two textbooks complemented our study: W. D. Maxwell's *An Outline of Christian Worship* and Brad Thompson's *Liturgies of the Western Church*.)

An enthusiastic study group can analyze the way its congregation worships and propose alterations or additions that might enhance the spirit of true worship. Some congregations even begin producing worship and devotional aids created by their more artistic and poetic members.

Out of this ferment, prayer groups may develop to pray specifically for the success of worship. Imagine what this alone can do to heighten the sense of expectancy as the congregation enters the sanctuary on Sunday morning! Anyone who has taken part in an all-night prayer vigil for a series of special services well remembers the high state of devotion and excitement with which he or she then attended the meetings. The same is true for people seriously engaged in prayer for the regular Sunday morning services. They come into the services standing on tiptoe for the miracles of God.

Whole Parts

A truly memorable worship service is one in which the particular prayers, hymns, anthems, responses, readings, sermon, and Communion all serve as points of entry for the overall experience. That is, the whole experience of worship is greater than the sum of the parts — so much greater, in fact, that there can be no comparison.

The parts contribute to the *order* of the service, but they never should restrict the *spirit* of the service. Because they are only ingredients, they never should disallow room for spontaneity or the coming of the Spirit.

Worship errs, on the one hand, when it lacks the proper ingredients, depending entirely on the movement of the Spirit. It also errs, however, when it's too rigid, foreclosing the hope that the Spirit will transform the situation into something unplanned and unexpected.

We see the former problem illustrated in many loose-knit services, whose lack of liturgical integrity or forethought repels persons of disciplined understanding and intellect, while the latter problem is all too familiar among churches with a tradition of highly liturgical orders.

I conceive of the discrete parts of the liturgy as building blocks whose purpose is to point us not to themselves, but to God, the One for whom all worship is conceived. When I remember this, I'm far less prone to idolize the liturgical parts themselves.

As ministers, we work diligently at preparing the parts of the service for which we have primary responsibility. We want the choice of hymns and anthems to be sensitive and informed, the prayers to be carefully framed and articulated, the sermon to be well conceived and artfully produced, and the Communion to be thoughtfully and appealingly offered.

But, even more, we want each part to be infused with prayer and surrendered to God as an oblation fitting for his service.

Thirty years ago I heard Elam Davies, the former pastor of Fourth Presbyterian Church in Chicago, say that he always spread on his desk or sofa the pages of a new sermon and prayed, "Here they are, O God, the best that I can give you." He made a deep impression on me. Everything we do — the preparation of worship as well as its execution — should be an offering to God.

If this is true for both pastor and people in worship, the separate items of the liturgy become a holy dance in which we whirl round and round with the Spirit. Something truly miraculous happens — a theophany.

The Dream of Substance

A few months ago a television executive confided to me the substance of a dream he had had about our worship.

It was the time of the offering, he said. But when I called for it, instead of a sober moment in which ushers passed among the pews extending the offering bags, there was an electric happening in which the people themselves poured into the aisles, crowding into our capacious chancel.

"They were everywhere," exclaimed the man, "all around the pulpit, up by the altar, filling the chancel, crowding around the steps, and choking the aisles! And they were kneeling! *They* were the offering. They themselves were the holy oblation. You were passing among them, touching them in love and blessing. And the sense of majesty filling our building was awesome, simply awesome."

I called this "the substance of a dream."

It is also the dream of substance — worship as worship ought to be, when, filled with a sense of the Holy One, we're all brought to our knees in humility and devotion.

For worship leaders, Sunday seems to come every three days. Trying to bring freshness and newness to worship constantly challenges us.

— *Howard Stevenson*

CHAPTER TWO
Arranging the Pieces

When I was on the faculty at Westmont College in Santa Barbara, I frequently drove to the campus on my Honda Gold Wing touring motorcycle along a beautiful, seven-mile stretch of the California coast. Dramatic cliffs and rocks lined the beaches; palm trees arched their spindly trunks in the sand; sailboats bobbed in the gentle blue-and-green swells.

I frequently reminded myself not to take this magnificent part of the world for granted. Each day I tried to see things I had not noticed before or to see things in a new way. For seventeen years I continued to marvel at the patterns and nuances of God's handiwork.

Leading corporate worship is like that beautiful commute: the challenge is to discover continual enjoyment in an oft-repeated exercise. "Worship is the adoration and praise of that which delights us," writes John Piper. "We praise what we enjoy, because praise completes the enjoyment. We worship God for the pleasure to be had in him."

How can we combat the propensity to let the heaven-directed activity of worship fall into dullness and routine? How can we do justice to this exalted calling when it falls to us to plan and lead it week after week, year after year?

For worship leaders, Sunday seems to come every three days. It's like a voracious animal that consumes all our efforts and then wants more. Trying to find freshness and newness in worship constantly challenges us.

On the average, I spend the equivalent of an entire working day each week in worship planning. I continually carry ideas around in my head. Special celebrations like Easter, of course, require months of planning. And choir anthems and the contributions of special-music groups are planned weeks in advance. But as a general rule, at the beginning of every work week, I begin to pull together the pieces for the next Sunday.

Here are some of the procedures I have found helpful as I plan a worship service.

Finding the Focal Point

I prefer to center worship around a theme — a focal point or central idea that gives the service sequence and depth. Sometimes the theme is supplied by the season of the year: Advent or Lent or Easter or Thanksgiving. Other times a special emphasis of the church, like a Missions Month or Family Sunday, suggest worship themes.

Of course, the sermon topic is a natural focal point. If the topic happens to be "God's Faithfulness" or "The Love of God" or "God's Sovereignty," it is not difficult to blend the hymns, anthems, and the spoken word with the sermon.

My pastor, Chuck Swindoll, and I communicate weekly about his sermon plans. Our memos and conversations include (a) sermon title, (b) passage of Scripture, (c) central thought, (d) key words or phrases that might be repeated or underscored in the message, (e) songs and hymn texts that have come to mind in his planning and preparation, and (f) other worship ideas or suggestions from him.

Then again, sometimes it's asking too much to know weeks and months in advance this detailed information. Also, it's not easy to highlight every sermon subject. I recall a three-week sermon series from Ecclesiastes that focused on various characteristics of "The Foolish Man." It's also difficult to coordinate worship and sermon when the preacher exposits Scripture verse by verse.

Consequently, over the years I've discovered the worship portion of the service can have a life of its own; it doesn't have to be connected with the sermon. This has been a liberating concept. Often, then, I let the theme of the choir anthem become the theme of worship, and I fit the other parts of worship into it.

In any case, when we focus on one theme, people can come to the end of thirty minutes of worship drawn together and to God.

Listing the Worship Resources

After determining the focal point of worship, I take a yellow pad and begin to list all the available resources for that theme.

First, I turn to four or five hymn books that I keep by my desk. I go to the topical index and the Scripture reference index, and I list all the hymns that might contribute to the theme of worship.

It matters not whether the song is known to our congregation, because a hymn can be used in several ways. It can be paraphrased in prayer, read by the congregation, recited by the leader, sung to another tune in the same meter, used as a solo, or played by an instrumental musician.

Then I list all the appropriate worship choruses. The interjection of these memorized and more personal songs often adds a delightful note of spontaneity and freshness. I keep a list of song titles at hand to avoid having to go through ten or a dozen of the latest spiral-bound booklets.

Next, I read the Scripture text in several translations, versions, and paraphrases. I also use a topical Bible and a concordance, both of which help me locate related passages that can be used in prayer or during transitions in worship.

Still another helpful source of fresh language is related readings and poems. Several good sources are listed in the bibliography of worship resources at the end of this book.

Finally, I review the various means we have of presenting these items: the spoken word, the choir, a pipe organ, people who can read interpretively, soloists and instrumentalists, a readers group, handbells, children's choirs, and the congregation.

This exercise with the yellow pad almost always produces more material than we ever could use in one service, but the process of listing these resources helps stoke creativity.

Exploring All the Possibilities

As I plan corporate worship for a large body of people week after week, one principle I constantly remember is this: The higher the predictability, the lower the impact. Remember that daily drive along the Pacific to the college campus? Whenever I got used to it, I began to lose the impact of that beautiful sight.

So, I also look at each element of worship from different angles, to see how it might be approached freshly or arranged in creative combinations and yet with dignity.

For instance, with Scripture I ask myself: *How can it make a special impact upon these people who routinely sit in this room Sunday after Sunday? Does it always have to be read as a monologue? Can it be read responsively by two people? Can it be sung? Can it be read dramatically by a practiced readers team? Is this a conversation between one, two, four people? Is there a crowd involved that the choir could represent? Can the prophet shout or call from some distant vantage point in the room? Can different people in the congregation stand and proclaim God's Word from where they are?*

Once when we read the Parable of the Sower, we had four different voices each take one soil and read that portion and its interpretation. Another time the choir shouted, "Hosanna to the Son of David!" during a reading for Palm Sunday. Another time still, a "prophet" declared from somewhere in the organ chambers, "Prepare ye the way of the Lord; make straight in the desert a highway for our God!"

The text can be taken directly from a particular Bible translation or rewritten as a contemporary paraphrase. Or a variety of passages could be combined into a mosaic of Scripture. The options abound.

Sometimes we have combined Scripture and music. Once we sang "O God Our Help in Ages Past," and between stanzas we read portions of Psalm 90, from whence Isaac Watts received his inspiration. When we had finished, our organist played a simple, soft, slow, single-line reminder of the melody and text: "Our shelter from the stormy blast, and our eternal home." It was a special moment.

Likewise, prayer can be approached in different ways. Although normally one person prays publicly in our service, sometimes several people have led in prayer, one after the other, in turn praying prayers of adoration, confession, intercession, petition, and thanksgiving.

Once a husband and wife lead us in an almost conversational style of prayer. Jim started out in praise to God; then Carolyn interjected items of thanksgiving; next Jim picked up, "And, Lord, there are many in our church family who need strength for trials. . . ."

Still another idea: guided, silent prayer. Or how about two, three, or four different places in one service for prayer? Or, try taking a hymn that has just been sung and "pray the hymn," using the words of the hymn as the basis for the organization and content of a spoken prayer.

In sum, all the elements of worship can be looked at creatively.

After this exploration, I begin to design a sequence of events that has logic and flow. In doing this, I am reminded of the difference between a streamlined passenger train and a freight train. A freight train is just a number of cars of all descriptions, linked together but with gaps between. From within a streamlined passenger train, on the other hand, the cars are clearly connected. Passengers easily walk from one car to another even as it is moving at high speeds.

I want worship to be like a streamlined passenger train: intellectually, emotionally, and spiritually continuous. That type of service, I believe, engages people most meaningfully.

As I think about the placement of various events in the drama of worship, several key principles emerge.

Focusing Attention

I have learned to appreciate a plan that I inherited when I came to First Evangelical Free Church in Fullerton in 1980. Just before we begin worship, our people, in typical Southern California, Free Church style, are warmly greeting and talking to one another, both in and out of the sanctuary, or "worship center," as we call it. Though there is organ music, it is not, as in many churches, a signal for silence in the pews.

A few minutes before the stated beginning time, one of our pastoral staff comes to the platform to greet people, underscore some announcements, and then encourage people to examine the bulletin, open their hymnals, and collect their thoughts for worship. Then the organist draws the veil of quietness with thirty to forty-five seconds of musical accompaniment, perhaps employing a hymn that will be used, a related musical thought, or a short praise chorus.

Then worship can begin, but again, in a variety of ways. Sometimes we begin quietly with the singing of a simple chorus, sometimes majestically with brass and timpani, sometimes formally, sometimes informally, sometimes with an anthem, sometimes with a reading or a Scripture passage. But in any case, the mind and spirit are focused on the occasion at hand: worship.

Once we positioned one of our soloists six to eight rows back in the congregation and gave her a cordless, lapel mike. At a preplanned point, she started to sing while seated, without accompaniment, without music in hand, "Brethren, we have met to worship." After singing a phrase or two, she stood and continued singing as quiet support from the organ joined her. She slowly moved down the aisle to the steps and faced her brothers and sisters, encouraging them in song to "Love God supremely" and "Pray with expectation as we preach the living Word." As the song came to a close, she moved back to her seat, singing as she sat down, repeating, now a capella, "Brethren, we have met to worship / To adore the Lord, our God." All was quiet; no one dared breathe; we were brought face to face with the supreme privilege and responsibility of worship.

Remembering Content and Flow

After we focus people's attention, the rest of the service can develop in countless ways, but two overriding principles guide my planning: logical content and emotional flow.

We want the content of the songs, readings, and prayers to contribute to the theme that we have chosen. The task is to present a drama that unfolds in a reasonable sequence and helps us reflect on God, who he is, and our relationship to him.

I want people to discover why a certain hymn was chosen, what it contributes to the theme, why it was placed just there in the order of service, and how it relates to the Scripture just read or the prayer that will follow. Sometimes the pastor or worship leader can supply that connection; other times we assume the worshipers will discern it.

At the beginning I usually try to establish the supremacy of God as the object of *our* worship. The thrust is God-directed, corporate worship. The pronouns of songs here usually will be "we," "us," and "our."

Later in the service may be the occasion for a more personal expression. Then congregational songs often will use "I," "me," and "my," drawing people to focus on their particular and individual relationship with God. This part of the service may be quieter and more reflective.

Emotional development is important. The service should not be an emotional monotone, but one that offers a variety of intensity.

If everything is quiet, somber, or reflective, the service may tend to feel listless. If everything is triumphant and one grand climax after another, people may quickly tire.

I also want to avoid jarring emotional shifts. The continuity of worship should provide a natural flow from one part to another. Otherwise, the jerking from one mood to the next will distract people from worship. Even the smallest details can be distracting.

For example, if I intended to follow a prayer with a song, I probably would try to think of a refrain or chorus that most people know by heart. Then, instead of interrupting the prayerful atmosphere with an abrupt, "Please turn to hymn number 492," I would have the organist simply begin playing chord progressions to establish a key, and I would start singing, "I love you Lord, and I lift my voice. . . ." With a small cue or motion, I'd invite the congregation to join in. In addition, I often put such songs in a lower key, so people, in a quiet mood, don't have to sing so high.

Keeping It Personal

Unless we guard against it, worship can become mere performance, an impersonal presentation of words and songs. To counter this danger, I remind myself that, above all else, our worship must be authentic and personal.

Sometimes I like to lead worship from the floor of the sanctuary. That helps overcome that separation of performers and people that the platform can foster. Or we'll have people come from out of the pews to lead a portion of the service as I described above. Or we'll engage the congregation in some way.

Not long ago, Chuck was preaching a series on Great Questions — things asked by Jesus and asked about him. One week, the question was, "Who is the greatest in the kingdom of heaven?" Jesus, of course, used a child to make his point.

I led some songs from the piano, and after we'd been into the service fifteen minutes, I had three children come forward. We talked about what Jesus thought of children, and I asked one of the girls to read the Scripture. I talked about some qualities of children that we never want to lose touch with: trust and the willingness to let others help. I also said we never want to lose the songs of childhood. Then the kids and I sang "Jesus Loves Me." A little touch like that helps make the service more personal.

Encouraging Participation

Sometimes people come to church and feel like they're watching worship instead of actually worshiping. We counter "spectatorism" by giving people plenty of opportunities to participate — songs, readings, and prayers — and by using nonprofessionals for different parts of the service.

If a lay person stands from the pews to read a proclamation, in a sense everyone does it. Any time we move the participation away from the pulpit and professional staff, worship is no longer a show but a common undertaking of leaders and people.

We do the same when we involve people's hearts as well as their heads. I'm convinced there are too few points of genuine inspiration in most of our lives.

I'll always remember the words of one man who asked to sing in our choir. "You know why I want to sing in the choir?" he began. "I'm an engineer, and I work with things I can measure, weigh, and feel. I'm inclined to take my spiritual life in much the same way — an inventory of knowledge and a cerebral concept of my Christian life. I need to learn to express the *emotion* of the Gospel."

He was onto a great truth: we have an inner need to experience worship, not just to watch it.

We Worship a Creative God, Forever

We seek variety, not for its own sake or because we want to put on a good show, but because we serve a God of infinite variety. We want to catch a glimpse of his face and his character from every possible angle. Each new revelation of truth and beauty and every expression of love and concern help us to understand him more.

I also like to remember that worship is the ceaseless activity of heaven — occurring right now as you read these words. One day, it will be our eternal activity.

Sometimes, I enjoy teasing Pastor Chuck by reminding him

that someday he will be out of a job. Preaching will be obsolete when we come into perfect knowledge. But worshipers will be fully employed forever, praising God. "O that with yonder sacred throng, / We at his feet may fall. / We'll join the everlasting throng / and crown him Lord of all."

So I strive week after week (every three days!) to plan and arrange worship in fresh and creative ways. After all, our practice of worship here on earth is perhaps our most significant preparation for the life to come.

A pastor, of course, must do many things to prepare to lead people weekly in worship, from preparing a sermon to putting hymnals in place. But before I attend to technical matters, I've learned to attend to spiritual concerns.

— *Jack Hayford*

CHAPTER THREE

Preparing Myself

I was 22 when I took my first pastorate, a small congregation in Fort Wayne, Indiana. At best we averaged forty-seven people in worship.

We had one rough stretch. As some members moved and others went away for the summer, our average attendance over a five-month stretch dropped steadily, from forty-seven, to forty-four, to thirty-three, to twenty-two, and finally, by the middle of August, to eleven.

One Sunday morning there were only eight people in church.

When my family came back for the evening service, nobody showed. No one.

I sat discouraged in the front row next to Anna, my wife, and our baby, who was lying in a bassinet.

I was already defeated after the morning service, but now I felt simply awful. *What in the world am I doing there?* I thought. If we had had enough money, I would have packed my family in the car and left town. But we didn't have it.

As I was sitting there, I made what I later realized was a crucial decision.

"Honey," I said to my wife, "you stay here with the baby and kneel. I'm going by myself to pray. If I we don't pray right now, this will beat us."

While praying I saw a mental picture of the church building on fire, not burning up, but flames were going up from the building, and the cinders blew east of the church and came down on top of houses and ignited them. I felt as if the Lord was telling me he was still intending to bring his "fire" to that church.

I was strengthened and encouraged to stay at the church, and did so for another two years. I can't say the church exploded with Spirit-filled enthusiasm after that. In fact, it never became much larger than it was at its peak. But in those two years, we had a number of families from that housing development to the east start attending.

That incident reinforced for me the priority of prayer in ministry and especially in preparing to lead worship. A pastor, of course, must do many things to prepare to lead people weekly in worship, from preparing a sermon to putting hymnals in place. But before I attend to technical matters, I've learned to attend to spiritual concerns.

What Distracts Us from Worship

Prayer helps my heart, mind, and soul focus on the meaning and direction of worship. I make prayer a priority because it dissolves the distractions of worship. My story illustrates a leading distraction: the yearning for superficial success. Certainly, I was concerned about the spiritual welfare of individuals at the time, but I confess I was also overly concerned with mere numbers.

But the yearning for "successful" worship can take other forms, each of which undermines our ability to lead worship in a right spirit.

1. Seeking a smooth service. During one recent Sunday service, I became angry. A group that was to make a special presentation didn't show up on time; it was a rainy day and the van that was supposed to bring them was late. I became irritated and said a couple of abrupt things to a staff member who was on the platform.

But immediately, I felt rebuked. First, I realized that this group's tardiness wasn't anybody's fault, certainly not the staff member's. Second, I remembered that the strength of our service isn't in its smoothness; that isn't the source of its power. So I quickly turned to my colleague to whom I had spoken harshly and apologized.

Naturally, we want a smooth service. If things are disjointed, people can be distracted from focusing on God. But spiritual power in worship doesn't come from the smoothness of transitions.

2. The pursuit of excellence. Sometimes we get distracted from true worship by being preoccupied with the excellence of the choir, the preaching, or the special music. We even sanctify that yearning by saying that nothing we do for God should be less than excellent. Unfortunately, we sometimes end up sanctifying human pursuit of excellence as though it somehow ennobles God.

The greater truth is that while we ought to aim for excellence, God doesn't need our excellence; it doesn't enhance him a bit. It may make things more lovely, but it can also lead to pride. We become preoccupied with style rather than substance, with how things look and feel rather than with what truths they communicate.

Naturally, I'm not encouraging a studied shoddiness to keep us all humble. From how we dress to how we lead singing, from how we make transitions in worship to how we preach, our worship leaders strive to lead to the best of their God-given abilities.

When the choir does well, for instance, we rejoice and are moved deeply. That's perfectly in order, as long as everybody keeps it in perspective.

3. *Longing for an effective service.* Sometimes we're distracted from worship because we want to make an impact on people. Perhaps in the first service I will say something funny that I didn't plan, but which nonetheless makes a point in the sermon. I may be tempted to repeat it in the second service mainly because it's cute or clever and people will like it. If that's my motive, the spiritual vitality will be drained from it.

Recently, in the first service, as I came to the key point in the sermon, I became increasingly moved as I spoke. I asked if we wanted to be a charismatic entertainment center or a body that transmits the life of Jesus to the next generation. I was surprised, in fact, at how moved I became. And I did something unusual for me: I hit the pulpit — hard!

I haven't done that ten times in twenty-one years of pastoring, yet on this morning, I did. But it came naturally, spontaneously, and it genuinely communicated my passion for the subject.

But what was I to do the next service? For me to mimic that emotion would be disastrous. To do so would be merely to seek an effect, an emotional response, and not to focus attention on the truth of the message.

By the time we enter the ministry, we've been made conscious of style and technique, intonation and appearances. Those are valid concerns. The machinery of worship is not unimportant. But when we end up being unduly conscious of such things, when they preoccupy us, we are distracted from the worship of God.

Attitude Check

It's not only poor technique that gets in the way of worship, but also improper attitudes. Developing a worshipful attitude is, for me, the most important thing I can do to prepare for worship. It's vital for me to nourish a real humility before God and to sustain a genuine childlikeness before the people I lead.

Unfortunately, our culture tends to think there is something fundamentally immature about childlikeness. But we in the church know there's a difference between childlikeness and childishness. *Childlikeness* is the attitude I want to nurture. It reminds me that no matter how old or seasoned I become, however mature or expert, when measured beside the Ancient of Days, I'm not that wise or experienced. I'm a mere child, not only at living the Christian life, but especially in leading others in worship.

In addition, I stress the importance of *childlikeness* because I want to remain flexible, open to the Spirit as a child is open (usually!) to the leading of loving parents.

As I suggested earlier, prayer is the key activity for me, especially when it comes to nurturing a childlike spirit. When I regularly engage in three particular types of prayer, I develop an attitude conducive to leading worship.

Putting My Spiritual Garden in Order

When I was a boy, each Friday night my father would give me a list of chores for Saturday. He usually worked on Saturday and wouldn't arrive home until after four o'clock. But then he'd walk with me and examine the work I'd done.

He was a perfectionist, although not an unkind man. He had been in the Navy where everything was ship-shape. So, he'd examine my yard work carefully. If I left a couple of leaves in a flower bed, he'd just point, and I would know to go over and pick them up. If he saw a weed I'd missed, he'd point it out.

For me this was a positive experience. I loved my dad, and I wanted to do well for him. When he looked at what I'd done, I wanted him to be happy. So when he pointed things out that I'd missed, I didn't mind. I would have done those things had I seen them, but I only saw them when he pointed them out.

King David wrote, "Search me, O Lord and know my heart. Try my thoughts and see if there be some wicked way and lead me in the way everlasting." When it comes to preparing myself for worship, that's my desire as well. I want my Heavenly Father to walk with me through the garden of my heart and see if I've missed anything.

I do this by regularly engaging in cleansing prayer. This is different from my daily devotions; it's more intense. Sometimes I feel like I need a thorough cleaning, like a car radiator periodically needs to be flushed. It usually happens about once a month. I take a day and devote it to prayer and self-examination.

I don't have a specific agenda. I usually prostrate myself and "call on the Lord," as the Psalms put it. I'm not loud, but since I'm alone, in a closed room, I feel free to speak aloud. I try to let God stir within me. I don't think I'm finished just because I feel stirred or teary-eyed. I'm ultimately looking for a new perspective on myself, a revelation of pride or self-centeredness, or an insight into what God would have me do next in ministry.

During one of these cleansing prayers, for instance, I was feeling a vague hollowness. I couldn't put my finger on a glaring sin, but eventually I realized I felt empty because I had been squandering my free time. It wasn't an earth-shattering revelation, but I had to acknowledge that I had been watching an excessive amount of television.

I see nothing intrinsically wrong with TV. It's just that there are few constraints to watching it. And it doesn't demand anything of me. In short, if I watch it too much, I begin to get lazy. I also enjoy reading novels and playing basketball, and these are activities that truly refresh me. I felt like the Holy Spirit was prompting me to prune this form of sloth.

So, regular cleansing prayer keeps my spiritual garden in order. It helps me maintain attitudes that allow me to lead worship in Spirit and truth.

Getting in Touch

For me, Sunday morning starts on Saturday night, and Saturday night begins with a special form of prayer. Almost every Saturday night about 7:00 or 8:00, I go to the church, walk through the sanctuary, lay hands on each chair in the room, and pray.

Sometimes I'll walk down every row, sometimes I'll go down every other, but I'll let my hand at least slide over every seat. Once in a while, I'll sing a hymn or chorus as I walk. Sometimes I'll do this alone, other times with a few church leaders. Praying through the sanctuary usually takes about fifteen to twenty minutes, but it makes a profound difference in the next day's service. Specifically, it does three things.

1. I become open to God's power. Although God is present with me at all times, when I acknowledge his presence and get in touch with his power, I become more dependent on him.

As I walk along, I might pray, "Lord, you've given me gifts as a speaker. But I also know I can't touch all those people where they need to be touched. Only your Spirit can touch their spirits. I ask you to do that tomorrow."

Sometimes I will so feel the presence of God, I'll be moved to tears. Other times I won't feel a thing. At such times, I go to the back of the sanctuary afterwards, look over the room, and pray, "Lord, I am glad that you're here, even though I don't feel one thing. And I'm depending on you being here tomorrow."

2. I allow the Spirit to lead. As I pray through the sanctuary, I'm also asking the Holy Spirit, "What is the one thing you most want to do tomorrow?" By this time, we have the essential outline of the service put together, but without the final details. So, it's a time when we can still adjust and decide which element of the service we will highlight. That decision, then, flows from this prayer time.

In our tradition, a "word of prophecy" is a message from God for the present moment. So sometimes as I'm praying this prayer and walking along, I literally will feel grief for people who have been bereaved. Another time I'll feel weepy for sick people. Yet another time, I'll become angry at Satan's attacks that have divided homes, abused children, or encouraged drug abuse.

I believe that these feelings are more than coincidence; they're burdens that the Spirit gives me. Naturally, they arise out of a complex set of factors: what I've been reading, who I've been talking with, what I've just seen on the news. But in the end, I believe the Spirit focuses these concerns and gives me a specific emphasis that should be woven into the next day's service.

Often, based on this experience, I will return home and re-write the introduction to my sermon or the opening remarks of the service. I'm not talking about changing radically any part of worship at this point. It's more a matter of bringing an emphasis to certain parts.

People have told me that I have a knack for opening sermons, for getting people's attention. If that is true, I attribute it to these times when I walk through the sanctuary, pray, and literally place my hands on the chairs where individuals will be sitting the next day, spiritually standing with them, identifying with their lives and need.

3. I impart a blessing to people. I also believe that in some personal way I impart a blessing to people by touching the seats and praying. It's not magic. I believe that, along with prayer, the Holy Spirit uses physical means (like human touch or bread and grape juice, for instance) to communicate himself to others. I don't speculate on how God does it, and I would strongly guard against any superstition that such a truth could breed. But I've found that God often integrates the visible and invisible realms to communicate himself.

We regularly receive letters from people who have visited our service. They say that as soon as they walked in the door, something began happening within them. They immediately sensed the presence of the Lord. What changed their life was not the smooth service or dynamic preaching, but their conviction that God was present in a special way when they were here. I believe that our Saturday night prayers are part of the reason people feel that way on Sunday morning.

In the same way, the night before a baptismal service, I'll often go to the baptistery, get down on my knees to reach into it, and stir the water with my hands as I pray. I believe the Lord wants to make every baptistery like the pool of Bethesda — a place where people are delivered from the crippling effects of sin.

There is, of course, no handy formula, no set prayer that will guarantee spiritual results. Praying over the chairs on Saturday night is not a third ordinance. But for me, it has been a practice that has borne spiritual fruit on Sunday morning.

Praying the Sermon

On Sunday morning, I, like many pastors, pray in preparation for worship. And this prayer takes a different form still: I pray through the sermon. Sometimes I look at notes as I do, but most of the time I simply think the thoughts of the sermon and pray about each one.

This has a homiletic aim, of course. It's one way to get the sermon firmly fixed in my mind. But for me the spiritual goal is more important. I liken the process to Elijah stacking the wood at the altar. What I'm doing in my study is stacking wood, and I'm asking for the fire of the Lord to come down upon the message and the congregation. I often pray something like, "Lord, I want to enter the service with my thoughts fresh and clear. And especially I want you to glow within me."

Often it's during this prayer that a fire for the heart of the sermon is ignited within me. One Sunday I was praying through my sermon based on the woman at the well. The subject was missions, and the main text was Jesus' statement: "Whoever drinks this water will never thirst again." I was feeling a little empty because it seemed such an obvious thing that people need Jesus to never thirst spiritually again. Ninety-eight percent of those attending the service already believed in Christ. I didn't want this to be a sermon only to people outside of Christ.

As I was praying, suddenly I was stirred with the thought that many in the body of Christ, even though they know him, still go back and drink at the old watering holes. They find, of course, that it's no more satisfying than before. But the reason they go back is because they've become preoccupied with their own thirst. If they would seek their satisfaction by satisfying other people's thirst, they wouldn't be thirsty for the things that used to attract them.

I can't convey in print what a difference that made in the service, but it became a powerful point in the message. It helped people identify with the woman at the well and to recommit themselves to satisfying others' needs and not just their own.

Leading Worship and Worshiping

One distraction happens not before, but during worship. During the service, there are a host of technical things to think about: how to make a smooth transition from one chorus to the next, when and how to get people to interact, how to signal the instrumentalists to cut a song short, knowing when and how to modify a sermon. The worship leader has so much to think about; there's hardly opportunity to worship personally.

At one level, of course, that can't be avoided, especially for the younger minister. For the first few years of leading worship, maybe pastors ought to make sure their need for worship is fulfilled in other settings, such as private devotions or visiting other churches.

But before long, you learn both to lead worship and worship. Some of that is due to experience. And some is due to the thoroughness of preparation. The more you've got the details of worship fully in hand, the more it is possible to operate on these two tracks at the same time: leading *and* worshiping.

It's like the concert pianist. He's practiced the piece, worked thoroughly on technique, and memorized every single measure. When he steps on stage, he keeps all this preparation in mind. But because his technical preparation has been thorough, he will also be able to be engaged fully in his playing. He will be recalling the various details as he moves through the piece, but he's doing more than playing a series of notes with certain physical techniques. He's personally involved in playing it with feeling. In some sense, then, he is able to enjoy the music more than the audience, which has not put as much into preparing for the performance.

Likewise, the worship leader, especially if he or she is well-prepared about the details of worship, can function on two tracks, with the spirit worshiping the Lord and with the mind thinking about what's coming next.

Even more important than technical preparation, however, is prayer preparation. When that's been thorough, the worship leader feels less like the pianist in control of the concert than the piano that is being used to play something beautiful and majestic.

Frankly, there are many times I feel like that. I've planned where I want the service to go, but then I'll make a change. It may be a change I've anticipated, but I will make the change because I feel prompted to make a change; for instance, I'll sense I should use one chorus instead of another. Certainly, my years of experience have helped me perceive some of these things. But I also believe that the Lord often prompts these changes. And during those weeks when he has rid me once again of pride, sin, or self-centeredness, I am open and can respond to his leading.

So, there's a greater freedom in worship when I'm thoroughly prepared, and not simply in things technical. It's especially important to Spirit-led worship, worship in which God's power is experienced, that I be prepared spiritually. And that has happened through various forms of prayer.

Distractions Diminish as We Get Older

I've noticed that I've gotten less distracted from true worship over the years. That's encouraging.

When I was younger, I fought spiritual battles I just don't have to fight anymore. I can remember times where I'd struggle with carnal indulgence or a bad temper, or when I idled away my time (for a while, I simply didn't take studying seriously).

I also used to feel a heaviness on Saturday night. I would dread the weekend. The first years of my ministry, I thought that was something ministers were supposed to feel, a burden the Lord imposed on his servants. I later realized that I was simply afraid no one was going to show up on Sunday. I was afraid all my preparations would be wasted.

But over time, God has helped me overcome in many areas. Certainly, I still struggle. For instance, I still feel spiritually weak sometimes — I feel I'm worth two and a half cents, on a high market day! But now it doesn't take as long to pray out of that kind of depression. That's nothing to boast about, of course; it's just part of the normal process of maturation in faith.

So, I've found that in preparing worship week after week, year after year, a lot of things become easier. It's not just that I'm preparing this Sunday's worship service; I've lived this way for thirty years. And it's not just experience, though obviously that has something to do with it. It's also easier (though not necessarily easy) over the years to prepare myself in the most important way, increasingly putting myself out of the picture trusting in the Holy Spirit.

PART TWO

The Service

Although the chancel choir, the soloists, and the instrumentalists are all vital contributors to the music of worship, our most important choir is made up of the men and women with untrained voices who sit in the pews.
— *Howard Stevenson*

CHAPTER FOUR
Keys to Congregational Singing

One of the most magnificent and impressive "choirs" I ever heard had never rehearsed. It was the vast audience that gathered in Anaheim Stadium one night during the 1985 Billy Graham Southern California Evangelistic Crusade.

I had been selected as the chairman of the local music committee and so assisted in the recruitment and direction of a 10,000-voice crusade choir, the largest crusade choir ever assembled in North America, according to Cliff Barrows. A magnificent sea of voices stretched along the entire third-base line.

Yet as mighty and moving as that choir sounded, the most powerful music that night came not from the third-base line, but from the huge, 85,000-seat stadium.

The sound still echoes in my mind, a memory that remains electrifying and overlaid with emotion to this day. As Cliff was leading the stadium in singing the gospel song "At Calvary," I slowly walked out to center field, behind the platform at second base, and standing in the middle of the stadium, I watched the moon rising over the second deck as the power of that great hymn cascaded over me.

"Do you hear this, Lord?" I heard myself saying. "Do you hear the praise of these people?" I was thrilled as I listened to the unified testimony and thanksgiving that filled the air.

To this day, whenever I sing the words of that hymn, I see again the image of that great, golden moon and hear those tens of thousands of voices singing: "Oh, the love that drew salvation's plan! / Oh, the grace that brought it down to man! / Oh, the mighty gulf that God did span at Calvary." I have spoken so often about that event that a friend framed those words for me, and I display them in my office.

That experience confirmed for me again the depth and impact of congregational song. It gathers strength in numbers and unlocks a deeper dimension of our souls, lifting our entire selves to God. Music is one key to the "heart dimension" of worship, whether we are gathered in a stadium, large church, hundred-seat sanctuary, or home Bible study. Singing has the power to help us freely express our feeling for God.

That's why an important part of our task as worship leaders is to involve the entire congregation in the ministry of music. Although the chancel choir, the soloists, and the instrumentalists are all vital contributors to the music of worship, our most important choir is made up of the men and women with untrained voices who sit in the pews.

Obstacles to Effective Singing

Effective congregational singing doesn't happen automatically whenever people gather. Consider some obstacles we face.

1. *A shrinking body of commonly accepted congregational song.* On occasion, when I have directed music at another church or conference, I have begun leading a hymn I assumed was a familiar song, expecting the audience to join in. Instead, I often have found that most of the group is unfamiliar with part or all of the song.

In some churches, unfortunately, the great heritage of hymnody, which represents the praise and prayer of the church of many generations, has been abandoned. At the same time, praise choruses, with a more transient life, have become popular. In addition, regional favorites may dominate a church's singing.

We live in a time when sacred music is more available than at any other time in history. Yet, ironically, our congregations are growing increasingly unfamiliar with our rich musical heritage, a heritage that could bind Christians together.

2. *A spectator orientation.* Singing, which can be such a joy, is fast becoming a spectator sport in our culture. Music has become something we listen to, not something we open our own mouths and participate in. For example, college music programs find fewer and fewer freshmen who are trained and experienced candidates for their school's choral offerings.

Having just entered my seventh decade, I recall my days as a youngster when I sat in the front row of a storefront Presbyterian church, singing hymns and gospel choruses at the top of my voice, singing every stanza and every part. And we sang outside of church, too. My public high school chorus was filled, and our rehearsal was listed as part of the regular weekly schedule of classes. It was a natural part of growing up to learn melody and harmony — soprano, alto, tenor, and bass.

My upbringing may have been a little unusual, but it would be nearly unheard of today — the age of Walkmans, concerts, video and audio cassettes, compact disks, FM radio, and ever-present headphones and speakers.

The proliferation of these spectator media makes me sometimes wonder, *How will the next generation ever learn to sing?*

3. *Misunderstanding the role of music in worship.* In churches,

sometimes the power and efficacy of music is unconsciously belittled or underestimated. We've all seen music used as filler: "Let's sing a song while the latecomers are seated" or "We have a little more time; let's sing that last stanza again." Other times music is considered merely a warm-up act for the sermon.

When music is demeaned like this, worship is diminished and congregational participation undermined. People won't fully participate — heartfully, soulfully — if they see the leaders treat music as an appendage to worship.

We often don't ask or expect enough of the art of music. It can reach, touch, and move people in countless ways. Underestimating it is like using a genie, with nearly limitless power, merely to do a few household chores for us.

It's a joy for me to work with a pastor like Chuck Swindoll, a gifted communicator who also has a deep love and respect for the ministry of music. We sometimes receive comment cards (from visitors, I assume) that read, "Too much music. We came to hear Pastor Swindoll." But Chuck knows music is as essential to worship as the sermon is, so we give plenty of time to it. Whenever the congregation is singing, Chuck is never distracted, never reading his notes. He, too, is singing enthusiastically, modeling how singing should be regarded by all.

4. Lack of time. If a good sermon needs time to develop and drive home a point, so does authentic worship. Worship needs at least fifteen to twenty minutes to build. In our church, we normally devote thirty minutes to worship — congregational singing, special music, and Scripture readings.

In order to devote that kind of time, we strive to eliminate as many nonessentials as possible. We want to give maximum time to worship and congregational singing. We know sermonettes produce Christianettes, and we don't want to find out what shortened worship produces.

5. Poor acoustics. Strong congregational singing requires the support and encouragement of the room itself. Ideally, the room should capture and blend voices when people sing. Unfortunately, many sanctuaries are lacking in one way or another. In ours, for example, the quality of the sound varies from place to place and from service to service, especially when the room is only half full.

There are ways to compensate for various acoustical problems, but the technical dimension of acoustics is too complicated to go into here. Suffice it to say that it's an issue not to be ignored.

Creating a Comfort Zone

In music, as in most endeavors, there is strength in numbers. The average person in the pews is reluctant to project his or her own voice unless surrounded by a host of other voices. Most people don't think of themselves as singers, and they tend to be afraid of their voices. This can be a handicap in smaller churches. But with the right leadership, even this difficulty can be overcome.

One key is to create a comfort zone for the congregation, an atmosphere devoid of tension, where a spirit of warmth and friendliness pervades, where people are not embarrassed to "make a joyful noise to the Lord."

How do you create this kind of comfort zone? First, by your own personality. If you are friendly, warm, accessible, and confident, your congregation is more likely to respond in kind. I find that smiling often and speaking in pleasant, personal terms breaks down many barriers.

Second, by having proper accompaniment. People sing more confidently when surrounded and upheld by a full sound; they won't feel they "stick out." When strong accompaniment provides an introduction that clearly establishes the tempo, intensity, and key, people sing the first lines more boldly.

Choosing the right instrument to accompany also helps. It would be difficult to render the strength and majesty of "A Mighty Fortress Is Our God" with a guitar, or even two or three. On the other hand, a meditative response like "He Is Lord" would go well with the more intimate sound produced by guitar strings.

Third, by selecting songs, at least in the beginning, that are easy to sing and well-known by the congregation. A good hymn doesn't need much direction. Examine a great piece like "Holy, Holy, Holy," and you'll find a straightforward succession of quarter notes, a simple rhythmic construction. But within that disarming simplicity is the beauty, strength, and majesty of the piece.

Fourth, by putting some songs in a lower key. I find many songs in our hymnals are written a step too high. When I select a hymn, I scan it for high notes. I try never to force a congregation to sing any note higher than D or E-flat, or an octave plus one above middle C. If a song is written higher than that, I ask my accompanist to transpose accordingly.

Fifth, paradoxically, by giving people permission not to participate. For various reasons, some people hesitate to join in sometimes. Often, when I'm introducing a new song or chorus, I'll have the choir sing it through and then I'll say, "You may not know all the words yet, but feel free to join in and hum along. If you don't know the phrases, just listen to the words, because that's part of worship, too." Then we'll sing it two or three more times. When we give people permission simply to listen, they often gain the confidence to join in, and by the third set, most of the congregation is singing.

Sixth, by lightening the spirit of the group. This may mean injecting a little humor. However, humor can be tricky, even deadly if it falls flat or is misunderstood. We've all seen music leaders try to perk up a lackluster hymn by good-naturedly chiding the congregation: "That was really lousy, folks! Let's try it again." Or, "Let's smile when we sing, okay?" Or, "Think about the words." We walk a fine line whenever we scold or lecture the congregation, even in good fun. Some people can pull it off, and some can't. Those who can't usually only dampen a congregation's desire to sing.

Instead, I lighten the group spirit by moving to a song with rhythm and life. I often reserve a song such as "This Is the Day" for that purpose. I'll say, "Let me sing to you, and then you answer, phrase upon phrase." Then I'll begin, "This is the day," and the congregation will echo, "This is the day." And I'll continue "That the Lord has made," and go back and forth with the congregation, having fun with the song. A song like that can help people loosen up and relax, and they'll sing more heartily after that.

Joy is close to every other strong emotion, and once we've unleashed joy through our singing, we can move quickly as a group to any other emotion on the spectrum. We can be laughing one moment and deeply moved to compassion or touched with grief the next. If we've done our job in creating a comfort zone for joyful expression in song, the Holy Spirit has greater freedom to move among us, speak to us, and change our lives.

These are seemingly mundane concerns, yet they are crucial for powerful congregational singing. I see hymns as sacred folk music. Hymn-leading is not a place for technical artistry, but for simplicity, for enthusiasm, for involving everyone in the worship experience.

Capturing and Focusing the Mood

Many people live emotionless lives, at least on the surface. In the routine of life, few of us are touched at the deepest point of our spiritual selves. Music is an emotional art form, communicating much more than the message of the words. Sacred music especially taps into our deepest spiritual and emotional levels.

As a worship leader, I'm privileged to bring inspiration to people. My job is to take people to emotional and spiritual heights, to show them the vistas and ranges of their faith, to lead them beyond the merely cerebral level of Christianity.

I need to remember that people bring to worship a wide range of experiences, tensions, needs, and moods. One woman carries a heavy load of sorrow, the man next to her a burden of guilt. The family in the next pew had a shattering argument on the way to church. Behind them is a man thinking about a business deal that went sour, his wife, who is planning next week's dinner party, and their teenage daughter, who is daydreaming about her boyfriend. Worship leaders must find some way to focus the minds and hearts of these individuals so that, with true unity, they may lift their praise to God.

Congregational singing is one of our best tools for doing that. And visualizing worship as a funnel helps me channel that singing to a unified end.

The opening of the service is like the wide mouth of the funnel, wide enough to include the emotions and experiences of everyone in the congregation, whatever they are. So we begin with broad themes, with songs that deal with unassailable truths such as the power, sovereignty, immortality, and unchangeableness of God.

With each successive selection, as we move down the funnel, we narrow our focus more tightly to the theme or desired response of that service.

The selection of hymns has a powerful influence on the overall mood and worship experience. I like to think of the array of congregational songs as my toolbox. As a craftsman selects a hammer to drive a nail, and a screwdriver to set a screw, I use certain songs for certain tasks.

Some hymns fill us with religious awe: "A Mighty Fortress Is Our God." Other hymns touch us with the love of God: "Amazing love! How can it be that Thou, my God, shouldst die for me?" Yet other hymns quiet our hearts and call us to prayer: "Take from our souls the strain and stress,/And may our ordered lives confess/The beauty of thy peace." And still other hymns soften our hearts and make us receptive to God's Spirit: "Just as I am, I come, I come."

By the time we get to the narrow end of the funnel, we can insert deeply personal songs — songs that call for an individual response or make some deep subjective impact. This would be the place for "Have Thine Own Way, Lord," "Open My Eyes that I May See," or "May the Mind of Christ My Savior." Or we might choose two or three brief praise choruses that focus on our love for God — "Lord, I Adore You" or "I Love You, Lord, and I Lift My Voice to Worship You" — simple, expressive, personal songs that people can offer to God without opening a hymnal.

Congregational singing, even though it's done with hundreds of other people, can be a powerfully personal expression of worship. It can implant truths in the lives of individuals.

The point of the funnel is to draw in and unify the hearts of the congregation, to focus the emotional flow of the worship experience, to prepare us for the ministry of the Word, and to allow people to express their response to God.

A Checklist for Congregational Singing

Music ministry and juggling have this in common: you have to keep a lot of things in the air at the same time. Spiritual sensitivity, personal preparation, attention to group dynamics, thoughtful song selection, and full-bodied accompaniment are just a few of the ingredients that contribute to powerful congregational singing. Here's a mental checklist I use to keep our congregational singing effective.

— *Are the songs meaningful?* Every worship leader needs to have the gentle and engaging sense of an educator. When I occasionally introduce a song by briefly describing its history or giving a new perspective on the theme, singing becomes more meaningful for the congregation.

I use a hymnal with a good set of indexes. I use the topical index to match our song selection to the theme of the service. Hymns that refer to specific Scripture passages can be found in the Scripture-allusions index. When that passage of Scripture is read before, after, or even between verses of the hymn, the singing becomes more significant.

— *Am I enthusiastic?* I want to let people know worship is enjoyable. Excitement is infectious.

— *Am I cultivating eclectic tastes?* I try to vary my choice of music. Since people speak different musical languages, we give people a variety of ways to express their worship. We avoid an either/or approach to traditional and contemporary music. We try to be both/and. The simple and spontaneous praise songs can find a powerful counterpoint in the strength and steel of hymnody.

— *Am I avoiding the routine?* I want to keep worship fresh and alive. I'll use the metrical index to discover what familiar tunes will fit a new set of words (or vice versa). That's a great way to introduce new material and yet still have enough familiarity that people will participate.

Periodically, I'll teach the congregation a chorus that's not in the song book. Or we'll sing a capella. Or I'll sit at the piano, talk a little about the history of the song or tie its theme into the sermon, and then lead them into the song. Or we'll try something visual or dramatic to introduce a song.

— *Am I explaining enough but not too much?* The essence of

every art is understatement. I don't want to draw the congregation's attention to every clever seam in our program; we want it to appear seamless. Likewise, we don't explain the significance of every song, even though there is one. We let our congregation discover many of the nuances of our worship.

   — *Am I alert to the emotional energy of the congregation?* I continually monitor how well I'm doing at creating that all-important comfort zone, capturing and conveying the mood of the music, funneling our congregation, and drawing all of our people into a unified experience of worship.

   In the harmony of pitch, rhythm, and lyrics, the congregation comes together, breathes together, and feels together. There's something indescribably moving about a group of diverse individuals who become united by the Holy Spirit and energized by infectious enthusiasm, and then open their mouths and offer songs to God.

   I dearly love choral singing; nothing challenges me more. Nonetheless, over the years I've been convinced again and again that our most important choir is the one in the pews.

Our worship leaders don't make a god of harmonious worship, but we do want to lead a service that runs smoothly and in which the parts blend, because orderly worship is worship that most helps our people.

— Jack Hayford

CHAPTER FIVE

The Harmony of Worship

Ultimately, I don't know that God cares if our worship runs smoothly, but people do. For that reason, among others, I want to lead a harmonious service.

Although worship leaders should give their best to God, polished worship isn't necessarily worthy worship. God looks first for contrite hearts in the worshipers.

Yet, understandably, people expect a certain professionalism or quality in worship. Their standards have been shaped by television, where performances are well-timed and segments blend into each other with the audience hardly noticing. When people come to church and find services disjointed and haphazard, they are distracted from worship. They may dislike worship that is nothing more than a stylized production. But neither do they appreciate sloppy services fashioned in the cause of "spontaneous" or "spiritual" worship.

People have been created by God with a desire for order. Only in an ordered environment can we respond creatively and faithfully. Basketball is a joy to play and watch because it's bounded by rules that create order. Life is most fulfilling when bounded by the order of the Ten Commandments.

Disorder, on the other hand, undermines joy and meaning. For example, children raised within an emotionally unpredictable environment created by an alcoholic father or parents who constantly argue often struggle in school or remain psychologically troubled for years.

So, when worship is disjointed or disorderly, seeming an unconnected patchwork of activities, it leaves people uneasy. Disorder creates a barrier that makes it more difficult for people to praise and respond fully to God.

Our worship leaders don't make a god of harmonious worship, but we do want to lead a service that runs smoothly and in which the parts blend, because orderly worship is worship that most helps our people.

What Makes for Disjointed Services

Services sometimes falter simply because of unfortunate circumstances. A singing group doesn't show up on time. The microphone goes dead in the middle of the sermon. An usher drops an offering plate. We cannot prevent such accidents.

Yet many disjointed services are made so by the worship leaders themselves. In particular, two practices can put a service out of kilter.

• *Too much silence.* Silence can be a powerful means of worship — when it's purposefully included and people are prepared. But silence and "dead air" are two different things. Worship leaders would be wise to think about those parts of the service where "nothing" happens.

For example, in many services, after the congregation sings a hymn and before the pastor stands to make announcements or read Scripture, there is a noticeable break. Instead of the service moving smoothly from one part to another, it halts so that people stop their worship and begin asking themselves, *What's happening next?* If that happens at every transition in the service, worship jerks along.

That jerkiness can be prevented if, for the example just mentioned, worship leaders plan to move toward the pulpit during the end of the hymn. For me that means timing the last few bars of the hymn with my walk from my seat to the pulpit. When I first began ministry, I actually practiced this on Saturday nights. Although experience precludes practice now, I still think about what will happen at the end of every segment of worship.

Often this requires coordinating with other worship leaders. The choir director and I talk about the timing of my introduction and the beginning of the choir's anthem. When I say a certain phrase, the director knows it's time for him to move into directing position. If the piece includes a musical prelude, I'll give a hand motion behind my back to signal when to begin as I'm concluding my remarks, so that when I sit down, the choir begins singing.

Again, we're not trying to dazzle people with a smooth performance. We're simply trying to make worship an orderly and, therefore, meaningful experience for people.

Some dead time cannot be prevented, but it can be put to good use. After I've asked people to look up a passage of Scripture, it usually takes them a minute to find it. Sometimes that can become an awkward gap, filled only with the sound of rustling pages. If that's the case, I will use that time to repeat an announcement: "Incidently, while you're opening to that verse, let me reiterate that today is the last day to register for the marriage seminar." Or I will give background for the text: "As you turn to the verse, let me remind you of what comes before it."

● *Too much talking.* My goal is not to fill every moment with noise. In fact, too much talking also makes for disjointed worship.

Special music doesn't always need to be introduced. To say, "Jeff is going to sing this morning for us" or "Now the choir is going to sing" clutters the service with something people can figure out for themselves.

If we're going to introduce a segment of worship, better to talk about how it relates to the sermon or Scripture reading. Even then, people often will notice the connection without our waving it in their faces.

Other times, a simple gesture will say more than words can. While I'm leading a song from behind the pulpit, singing, let's say, "Holy Lord, most Holy Lord, you are worthy of our praise," I will move out from behind the pulpit. Just changing position can accent the verse or hymn we're singing in a way a verbal explanation can't.

Other times, after the choir sings an especially moving song, I'll move slowly to the pulpit, letting the impact of their song fill the room. Instead of saying too much — "Thank you choir for that wonderful piece. It was a blessing to hear a reminder of . . ." — I'll simply say a quiet "Amen" or nod at the choir in obvious appreciation.

Knowing when to talk and when to be silent comes with experience. Sometimes, in fact, the Spirit leads me during the service in ways I hadn't planned. But in most cases, it's not something that happens haphazardly. Under the Spirit's guidance, I trust, it's carefully thought out ahead of time.

The Harmonies of Worship

Leading harmonious worship begins with understanding what exactly we aim for.

● *Harmony of attitude.* If the words of worship describe God's acceptance of people but my attitude suggests I'm frustrated with them, worship will be out of tune. In leading worship, then, I try to communicate the love of God not only with the content of worship, but also by the way I lead it.

When we introduce the Lord's Table, for example, we don't flinch from recognizing that Jesus died on the cross; that nails were driven into his hands, thorns into his head, and a spear into his side; and, most importantly, that he died because of our sin. We thankfully acknowledge the sacrifice of Christ and humbly accept responsibility for our transgressions.

But I especially communicate, both with my words and my demeanor, that he died for us because he loved us, because we were treasured by the Father. So we partake of the Supper not with heads hanging low because we are unworthy (though we are), but with faces lifted high with thanksgiving, because he thought us worth saving! It becomes not a somber memorial of sacrifice, but a joyful celebration of new life.

● *Harmony of the parts of worship.* Over the years, I've become increasingly convinced that worship is more than a good sermon. The other parts of the service are not mere preliminaries to the main event of preaching. That view puts an imbalanced emphasis on the mind. Instead I see worship as a harmony of emotion, intellect, and will.

Worship includes the joyful praise of God, the serious listening to his Word, and the obedient response to his will, but not necessarily in that order. I've found it is better to mesh the sermon into the service, and the service into the sermon, calling for people's response at both times. Then, instead of the service seeming like two disconnected parts, it will be a unity that calls people, in both heart and mind, to respond to God.

The Sermon in the Service

The sermon will be better integrated into the service, and therefore into the lives of the people, if it is "preached" elsewhere than during the sermon slot. Here are some ways I do that.

● *Let the people start the sermon.* After I've greeted the people, I might say, "In a few minutes we'll look at 2 Peter, the third chapter, where the Bible says God is never deceived. We'll be looking at God's wisdom and how we can be made wise by it. As we greet one another this morning, say to each other, 'We serve a wise God' or 'God's about to make us wiser!'"

Another sermon centered on "Embracing the Truth," so we

greeted each other with embraces.

Doing this too often would get old. But many weeks, by the time the greeting is through, the people have already begun my sermon.

● *Pray the sermon.* Sometimes the sermon theme can become the theme of the church's prayer time. Recently, I was preaching on Jesus' statement, "You shall know the truth and the truth shall set you free." To introduce "ministry time" (the segment of the service when people gather in small groups to pray), I said, "People are bound by many things this morning. Some people here feel their backs against the wall financially. For some the bondage is physical; they feel bound by a disease or disability. Some people feel bound by marriage or troubles with children or parents. Let's pray for these and others, that the truth of God's promises will set each of them free from their particular needs."

Again, this wouldn't work if used every week. But occasionally it's a way to plant seeds for the sermon.

● *Give the first part of the sermon elsewhere.* Sometimes I use ministry time to introduce the sermon. I'll tell the opening story, for example.

One week I told of a humorous encounter I had with our garbage collector, and I took four or five minutes as I led into ministry time. Afterwards, I said, "When I mentioned meeting the garbage man in front of the house the other day . . . " and moved into the body of the message.

Others could use the time before the pastoral prayer or the Scripture reading in the same way. It not only frees up more time for the sermon, it integrates in another way the sermon and the service.

● *Warn people about controversial sermons.* If the sermon topic will be controversial or make people uneasy, it's likely to draw a great deal of attention. That will make the service seem unbalanced. So, when the sermon theme might dominate a service, I try to integrate it early into the service, and with a little humor if possible, thereby diffusing unwarranted surprise.

If I were to preach about sexual purity, for instance, I might say something like this at the greeting, "Incidently, this morning

I'm going to be dealing with the subject of sexual purity." Then I'll pause and ask, "How many people are wondering if they'd better get out of here right now?" The people will laugh, and I'd tie it into the greeting: "Greet each other with 'Wow! I can hardly wait to hear this sermon!' "

Sometimes, of course, humor is not appropriate, but people can still be forewarned. During Sanctity of Life Sunday, I let people preview the sermon in the invocation. I prayed, "We praise you, God, for your creative works, especially that you created each one of us." Then, speaking more slowly for emphasis, I said, "Today, Lord, we are mindful that we are part of a culture in which innocent human life is taken daily. So we come with repentance. But we also come with joy, knowing every single one of us has been given the right to exist and in Christ to find you, God, and to discover himself or herself fully."

The controversial sermon introduced early, then, will not stand starkly when it is preached.

● *Integrate to the end.* In our service, after the sermon, we're nearly done. But we don't want the service simply to trail off.

After the sermon, we take the offering and sing a closing hymn, and then I dismiss the people. But I dismiss them in a way that pulls together the rest of the service. I may send them off with a joyful exhortation to live their lives in a way the sermon suggested, such as, "As you leave today, love one another as Christ loved you." Or I may ask them to turn to one another and repeat a key phrase from the sermon.

Even if the service has been laced together neatly up to this point, I think it's important to tie it together at the end.

The Service in the Sermon

Although the sermon is a one-way street, the entire sermon time doesn't have to be. Here are some ways we integrate the response of the people into the sermon.

● *Have people repeat key ideas.* Sometimes in a sermon I'll ask people to repeat a phrase or verse I've just spoken. I might say, "The main point of this first paragraph of our text is this: God loves us without condition. Say that with me. . . ." In addition to reinforcing the sermon theme, this gives people a way to interact with me during the sermon, as they would during a responsive reading. It also helps prevent the sermon from becoming a long monologue.

I've had some people object when I do this, saying it's a technique for teaching children, not adults. But I've noticed that major corporations use it in their sales seminars and management training. It's a common practice because having students repeat key ideas helps them remember.

In the context of worship, it's also a way to help people participate in the sermon as an act of worship.

● *Have people reinforce the sermon to one another.* Once when highlighting the truth that, because Christ has made us righteous, all Christians can be called *saints*, I asked people to turn to one another and introduce themselves to each other saying, "Hello, my name is Saint ——," inserting here their first name. So people turned to each other and said things like, "Hello, my name is Saint Luke" or "My name is Saint Helen" or "My name is Saint Buddy." It drew a few chuckles, but it highlighted my point. And it got people talking to each other, so that afterward they were worshiping together.

● *Ask for commitment along the way.* Instead of waiting to ask people for a commitment at the end of the sermon or at the conclusion of the service, I'll sometimes ask for one or more commitments during the sermon.

If the sermon encourages people to be thankful for God's goodness, I might invite people to turn to each other and mention something for which they are especially thankful.

If I feel the middle of the sermon is reaching disturbingly into people's lives, I might say, "The Holy Spirit tells us that if we repent, he will change us. I sense some of you want to repent. Let's take a few moments to pray. Go ahead and tell him right now. Say, 'I am sorry God. Begin to change me even now.' "

After a few moments, I might move them to praise. "Now let's lift our heads and tell Jesus, 'Thank you for forgiving me and for your promise to make me new.' " And then I'll get back into the sermon. At that point not only have people had an opportunity to rededicate themselves and praise God, but I've been given a fresh start for the next part of the message.

As I've suggested above, such practices can be overdone. But when used wisely, they allow me to preach longer, rivet each point I make, and help people participate in worship while they listen to the sermon.

The Best Laid Plans Are Not Enough

I mentioned that one service I asked people to turn to one another and introduce themselves, saying, "Hello, my name is Saint ———." That exercise helped most people think about themselves in a new light. All except one man.

My wife Anna was sitting next to him. She turned and said to him, "I'm Saint Anna."

The man paused, and then said, "I can't say it."

Thinking him shy, she prompted him, "You don't have to feel awkward. Remember, we're saints because of Jesus, not ourselves."

"I know. I believe that firmly," he said.

"Well, just say it, then."

"No. I'm not saying it." Then he paused, smiled, and lowered his voice. "My name is Bernard."

This humorous incident reminds me that even with the best of planning, I'm not in charge of worship. I cannot guarantee everything I do will help everyone enjoy harmonious worship.

In fact, although some of our services tie everything together neatly under one theme, many deliberately don't. The main thing is that worship be tied together in tone, and that praise, teaching, and response weave through the hour.

When that happens, even if one or two parts don't go as planned for everyone, the service still has an effect, moving people to see and respond harmoniously to the love of God.

Worship is a vertical rite in which the individual is caught up in the very presence — feared, dreaded, or beloved — of the Deity. Thus worship is and must be prayer, for nothing short of communicating with the One being worshiped will suffice.

— John Killinger

CHAPTER SIX

The Place of Public Prayer

P reacher," said a man on the worship committee of one of my churches a few years ago, "I don't mean this personally, so no hard feelings, but I think about the most boring thing we do in our worship services is pray. Therefore I propose that we eliminate as many prayers from our services as we can and fill the time with other things."

A stunned silence settled over the meeting. "Bob," I finally said, "you may be right. I'm not going to respond without giving what you said some thought. Why don't we schedule a time when we can all talk about it at length?"

He appeared satisfied. After all, it was his first meeting with the committee, and he probably expected his suggestion to be shot down without dignity. Now, at least, his pastor had responded and promised to put it on the agenda for a later meeting.

I confess I did have an immediate response, even though I chose not to voice it that evening: *Man, you don't understand Christian worship at all! Christian worship is prayer. That's what our whole service is about. The hymns, responses, readings, offering, time of commitment — they're all a way of praying, of responding to God for his gracious gift to us.*

But I knew nothing would be lost by delaying the discussion. In fact, at least two things eventually were gained. One, I was prepared for a more generous, thoughtful discussion than we might have had that first night. And, two, Bob found time to come up to speed with other committee members. Upon learning more about the theology and history of Christian worship, he sheepishly admitted that, although his boredom in worship had been genuine, his specific suggestion had been out of order.

Worship Is Prayer

Theologically and historically, worship is prayer. Jewish synagogue worship, on which New Testament liturgy originally was based, consisted primarily of hearing scriptural readings and comments on them, and engaging in prayer and praise to the God of Israel. Early Christians added to this the congregation's celebration of the Lord's Meal. But they recognized they were in the presence of the Holy One of Israel and that they came together foremost to pray and to praise God.

Christian worship always has been, therefore, essentially an act of commemoration in which we reconsider God's benefits to us and make an oblation of ourselves to the God of our faith.

Most of the hymns we sing are prayers. Almost all our favorite hymns either are addressed directly to God or apostrophize God's greatness and mercy. Consider "Joyful, Joyful, We Adore Thee," "How Great Thou Art," "Dear Lord and Father of Mankind," and "I Am Thine, O Lord," whose very titles indicate direct address to the Deity, and "A Mighty Fortress Is Our God," "When I Survey the Wondrous Cross," and "O for a Thousand Tongues to Sing," which are all prayerful exclamations of our faith in God and delight in his redemption.

That we sing the hymns instead of saying them alters not the fact that they are prayers. The hymnal actually is a congregation's prayerbook and contains many of the finest prayers in our language.

Most services begin with an introit or an invocation — either one, a prayer. Then they unfold through various stages of communication with God, from the *approach* through the time of *recognition* or *confession,* through the *restatement of the Word* (God's communication with us) and the *offering* (our response to his Word), through *Communion* (if it is observed, which is further remembrance of God's communication) and the *departure to serve,* when the guidance and protection of the Holy Spirit are invoked for a final time. From beginning to end, the act of worship is an act of prayer, a convening of God's people to remember his mercy and to respond in prayer and self-giving.

Worship aims to unite the believer with the Deity. Worship is not a mere celebration, not a *horizontal* rite in which people relate to one another for sociological reasons; it is a *vertical* rite in which the individual can get caught up in the very presence — feared, beloved, dreaded, or eagerly awaited — of God.

Thus worship is and must be prayer, for nothing short of the act of communicating with the One being worshiped will suffice to accomplish this purpose.

Prayer: The Test of Liturgy

Herein lies the perfect test to see whether the various parts of the liturgy measure up as genuine components of Christian worship. We have only to ask of a hymn, a reading, a chancel drama, "Is it prayerful? Does it conduct worshipers into the presence of the Most High? Is it appropriate as part of the content of a service directed to God?"

I test even the sermon by such a rubric. We aren't accustomed to thinking of sermons in this way, for sermons, especially in their development in America, have had, more or less, a life of their own, apart from ritual and ceremony.

But if worship is indeed the act of coming before God, and if it is enacted as Søren Kierkegaard suggested, with God as the audience, then a sermon is out of place in worship when it does not breathe an air of prayer and sensitivity to the Deity's presence.

Suppose I prepare a sermon on a prophetic text such as Amos 4:15 ("Hear this word, you cows of Bashan on Mount Samaria . . .") and in the course of writing vent some personal anger against certain members of the congregation. Is such a sermon really appropriate in the setting of Christian worship?

The one sure litmus test is to ask, "Can this sermon, as I have prepared it, be given with a sense of prayer and devotion?" If it can, well and good. If it cannot, then I should alter or abandon it.

The fact that worship is prayer means we are obligated to be serious about what we say and do. We cannot merely play at worship, for that would involve us in the hypocrisy of which God accused the Israelites in the day of Isaiah: "The multitude of your sacrifices — what are they to me?" says the Lord. "I have more than enough of burnt offerings, of rams and the fat of fattened animals; I have no pleasure in the blood of bulls and lambs and goats. When you come to meet with me, who has asked this of you, this trampling of my courts? Stop bringing meaningless offerings! Your incense is detestable to me. New Moons, Sabbaths and convocations — I cannot bear your evil assemblies" (Isa. 1:11–13).

Robert McAfee Brown has suggested in *Spirituality and Liberation* that prayer — truly genuine prayer — leads to revolutionary transformations in ourselves and the world around us. We cannot consistently pray for God's kingdom to come on earth as it is in heaven, or for God's will to be done in our own lives, without eventually being shaken by the results.

I have long regarded the prayers of the liturgy — the formal, stated prayers — as my greatest opportunity for eventually subverting the selfish human will of the congregation and turning it to the purpose of God. While I preached only occasionally in my parishes on such great prophetic issues as our duty to the poor and homeless, our concern for victims of prejudice, our care for persons with AIDS, and our love for the enemies of our country and its ideology, I rarely missed an opportunity to pray about them.

Here, for example, is a pastoral prayer from my last year in a Los Angeles pastorate:

> O God, whose grace envelopes us now like an invisible mist, penetrating our bodies and permeating our minds, help us to relax and submit to the total therapy of your presence. Forgive the mistakes we have made, the wrong choices, the weakness of will, the lack of love, the rebellion of spirit. Let the Spirit who was in Christ Jesus be now in us, drawing us back into the way of obedience and love and sacrifice. Teach us how to find ourselves by denying ourselves and how to serve you by serving others. Bless the wandering souls who have come our way today in search of truth or fellowship or inspiration. Make yourself known, both here and in other places, to those who are open to your coming, to those who sorrow, to those who are dying, to those who feel alone, to those whose burdens in life are extremely heavy. Grant your peace to AIDS and cancer patients, and hope to their families. Let your loving protection surround our young people, saving them from the cynicism and immorality of our age. Inspire your servants in the media industry with a vision of your kingdom, that they may mold the public consciousness toward those things that edify and redeem a people. Imbue our president and his cabinet and the Congress of our nation with a continuing spirit of love and unselfishness, that they may work for a world in which no child goes to bed hungry and no elderly person sleeps in the cold. Hold this church before the cross of Jesus, that it may see the true dimensions of its calling and center not upon its edifice or its distinguished history but upon salvation through faith alone and loving service to the lowliest of the low. For you are the God of all humanity and the gracious Lord of all peoples. Amen.

I reasoned that, while people might well complain about a sermon dealing with their failure to follow the summons of Christ to love our neighbors, *all* of our neighbors, they hardly would be unhappy at my speaking to God about it. Apparently I was right. I've never been reproached by church members for speaking of even the most sensitive issues in a pastoral prayer.

And occasionally I've breathed a little prayer of thanksgiving upon hearing some church officer, who had once appeared hermetically sealed against the idea I was praying for, come out with a similar prayer on some public occasion. Then I knew that the fullness of the gospel was getting through!

Distinctive Prayer

But I haven't forgotten my friend Bob and his complaint that prayer is the boringest part of worship. Even though Bob came to a new view in the course of our committee meetings, his initial reaction reminds me of the response of many church members to the stated prayers of the liturgy.

So I do everything in my power to make these prayers as lively and interesting as possible. Otherwise many people simply will tune out during prayers.

Here are some guidelines I found helpful for infusing freshness and excitement in the set prayers:

• *Prepare your prayers in a spirit of prayer.* The Apostle reminded us that the Spirit of God prays for us at levels we cannot attain on our own (Rom. 8:26–27). I ignore this spiritual reality only to the detriment of my praying. Once I've felt the flow of the Spirit's power in my life, I can follow the flow as I prepare specific prayers. This makes it easier to follow the next suggestion.

• *Fill prayers with important matters.* This is not to say I should never pray about small matters. It often is helpful to mention the little grace notes in life, such as the beauty of flowers, the singing of the birds, and the sounds of children's playing. But I make these the accents to my prayers, while I concentrate on the great issues of redemption, renewal, love, justice, hope, and service.

I sometimes review my prayers of the past six months to see

which subjects they dealt with. The resulting list ought to include such grand themes as the gift of Christ's death and resurrection, the empowerment of his Spirit, our care for the poor and displaced, the achievement of justice in our courts and among the nations of the world, and a sense of love, forgiveness, and compassion in our relationships.

● *Be specific.* Prayers become real when they deal in the day-to-day applications of the above abstractions. Instead of praying for the poor in general, I try to pray for the homeless who pass my church each day. Instead of asking God to bless the earth, I ask for conscientious use of herbicides on lawns or fluorocarbons in hair sprays. The same message gets across, only more potently.

When I attended Lenten services at the Cathedral Church of the Advent in Birmingham, Alabama, I was startled and impressed to hear the cathedral's dean, Laurence Gipson, make intercession for the Alabama Power and Light Company and its employees. He did this for an entire week. Another week he prayed for the city government and its employees. The effect was galvanizing; I found myself mentioning them in my own prayers.

● *Employ biblical words and phrases.* This is one of the secrets of the Anglican *Book of Common Prayer*, of its endurance as a great devotional guide and its immense popularity across denominational lines. Thomas Cranmer, the spiritual genius most responsible for the *Book of Common Prayer*, echoed the Authorized Version of the Bible in almost every phrase and sentence of his masterpiece.

Today we're wise to use contemporary translations of Scripture in order not to sound archaic and funny to modern parishioners, but it's still a good practice to use words and phrases from the Psalms, the Gospels, and the Epistles. They ring authentic and serve to keep us on track with the great biblical ideas.

● *Block those clichés.* I try to go through every prayer and blue-pencil trite and overused phrases, substituting words that are lively, picturesque, and engaging. A cliché is *worn* speech, speech that has lost its ability to grab the mind, so that it slips through without making an impression.

People respond better to images that speak to the right side of the brain than to analytical language directed at the left side. A young intern at a church I attended in Nashville said in a prayer on a particularly cold winter's day, "O God, you are like a cup of hot chocolate to us on a day like this." The phrase was arresting, and many people commented on it.

● *Use strong, short words and employ as few adverbs and adjectives as possible.* Sometimes, I fear, we pray as if we feel that in addressing the Deity, we should sound learned and impressive. Unfortunately, using multisyllabic words we wouldn't use in everyday speech only makes us sound pompous and silly.

How simple are the words and phrasings in the Bible: "The Lord is my shepherd, I shall not want." "The fool says in his heart, 'There is no God.' " "Blessed are the meek, for they shall inherit the earth." I try to select strong and active verbs, always preferring those that convey a sense of power to those that are merely florid and high-sounding.

● *Vary the pace and rhythm by creating sentences of different lengths.* Nothing dulls people's senses faster than a sing-song manner of speaking that results from too many short sentences, unless it is the monotony of long, involved sentences with piled-up subordinate clauses. I break the lengthy sections of my prayers with short, stacca-to-like statements. Note the variety in this brief Communion prayer:

> At this table, Lord, we shed our pretensions about ourselves. We know we are sinners. We know we often fail in life — at work, at school, in our relationships, in our values, in our faith. But as you reached out to your disciple Peter and clutched him from the waves, reach out now to us and rescue us. Teach us how to see your presence here. Give us thankful hearts for the mystery of this food and what it means to our faith. Send your Holy Spirit upon us to illumine the way we should think and believe when we have eaten and drunk. And bind us all together in the fellowship of your love, from this moment forth and forever more. Amen.

● *Watch the tone.* I find it best to create a mood of holiness in prayers through what I say, not through "holy" language or the tone of my voice. A stained-glass voice is a poor substitute for a genuine sense of the presence of God honestly felt and simply addressed.

A mood of holiness often begins with the initial way God is addressed in the phrase of the prayer called the "ascription." Consider the following ascriptions:

> O Lord God invisible, who dwells in the light and yet is not seen by mortal eye . . .

> God of all mercy, whose wisdom has appointed us to our particular places in this life . . .

> O God, who broods over us at night like a mother bird over her nest and rises upon us in the morning like the sun that warms the earth . . .

> O God, who has been our refuge in the hours of the world's suffering . . .

Each ascription immediately reminds us of some special quality of God, and this calls us to an attitude of reverence.

● *Aim for a sense of "sacred intimacy."* If worship is to awaken and cement the bond between the individual and God, then prayers should be phrased to facilitate the exchange. The opening prayers of the liturgy especially should set this mood, reminding worshipers of the loving nature of God and initiating the process of conducting them into life-changing personal encounters.

Here are some examples of intimate prayers from various parts of the service:

> *Invocation:* O God of sights and sounds and truth and feelings, we praise you for the softness of children's flesh, the feel of the grass under bare feet, the sweet smell of summer rain on hot pavement, the abundance of flowers in the earth, the sense of worship in a place like this. Receive us now, rich in things but poor in soul. Set us on your knee like little children. Hear the humble prayers we make and the songs we sing. And renew us for life in your beautiful world. Through Jesus

Christ our Lord. Amen.

Confession: I admit to you, O God, that I am often distressed by the daily news: by the failure of nations to agree, by the insistent problems of hunger and war and economy; by crime and negligence and immorality. I wish that my sense of the presence of Christ were stronger and that I had more confidence in his eternal victory over the world. Then I would not be shaken by the winds of adversity, but would stand like a tree planted by the living waters. Forgive my weakness, O God, and deepen my faith in your Word. Through Jesus Christ. Amen.

Offertory: The cattle on a thousand hills are yours, O God, and the diamonds in a thousand mines and the oil in a thousand wells. So are the homes we live in and the land we live on and the income with which we buy our food. We thank you for what we have by sharing it now with others in the world, through the work and ministry of this church and your kingdom. Amen.

● *Prime your pump with selections from volumes of published prayers.* Sometimes I have a hard time getting started on the preparation of prayers, even after waiting before God in a mood of meditation. That's when others' works can help.

I resist the temptation to borrow the prayers outright, for this short-circuits my creative powers, impedes my growth, and lessens the chances that the prayer will be suited for my congregation. But a phrase or an idea from someone else's prayers may well become the spark that ignites my generative ability and starts me on the way to a prayer of my own.

A Texas minister I know keeps a well-worn copy of John Baillie's *A Diary of Private Prayer* on his desk for this purpose; and when I once questioned William Sloane Coffin about a similarly worn volume of E. Lee Phillips's *Prayers for Worship* on his desk at Riverside Church, he said he'd found it indispensable for getting his own prayer compositions going.

In the pastorate, I kept several other excellent collections at my elbow: William Barclay, *Prayers for the Christian Year* (SCM, 1964); Horton Davies and Morris Slifer, *Prayers and Other Resources for Public Worship* (Abingdon, 1976); Arnold Kenseth and Richard P. Unsworth, *Prayers for Worship Leaders* (Fortress, 1978); Samuel H. Miller, *Prayers for Daily Use* (Harper and Brothers, 1957); and Leo S. Thorne, ed., *Prayers from Riverside* (Pilgrim, 1983).

• *Surround prayers with a context conducive to prayer and praise.* I've visited churches in which the liturgist related a number of announcements and then said, somewhat abruptly, "Let us pray." Since prayer is usually a mood before it becomes an actuality, such treatment may preclude anyone's experiencing the mood.

I derive much more from a prayer if it is introduced by a moment of silence or soft music, or even if it is preceded by the reading of Scripture. Carlo Caretto tells about his practice of going into the desert for an hour or more before entering the sanctuary to pray. Even a brute, he says, should compose himself before going to God in prayer. That is a good rule for public worship as well as for private devotions.

• *Leave pauses and silences for private prayer within the public liturgy.* "Be still," says the ancient text, "and know that I am God" (Ps. 46:10). Our Quaker friends long have understood the benefit of creative silence in the midst of worship, a gestative time in which worshipers may listen to the voice of the Spirit in their hearts. Because many of our people are unskilled in the use of silence, they tend to become bored or anxious when left to their own devices. But the gradual introduction of such moments can help us remember the God we adore is the *Mysterium tremendum* as well as the Father of our Lord Jesus Christ.

Boring Prayers?

Are prayers boring in worship? Not if worship leaders aren't bored with their relationship to God and the prospects of worshiping him. Our prayers ought, on the contrary, to be the most exciting moments in the agenda of worship, for they are the moments when it is easiest to break through the veil to eternity and whisper into the ear of God.

We have only to instruct our congregations in the true meaning of worship, so that they see the liturgy from beginning to end as a spiritual service, and then to pour our best efforts into the formation of the prayers. God, who hears from heaven, will answer in ways that will astound us.

Prayers in this chapter appeared originally in *Lost in Wonder, Love, and Praise: Prayers and Affirmations for Christian Worship*, Angel Books, 1986.

This continues to be one of the greatest challenges in church music: not only to perform the masterworks with authenticity and integrity, but also to choose and present the simple song or the prayerful response in just the right way.

— Howard Stevenson

CHAPTER SEVEN

Coordinating Other Contributors

A well-rounded worship service will allow people to express their individual gifts. Some can sing solos beautifully; others are trained at keyboard or orchestral instruments. Still others can perform drama or read Scripture effectively.

Yet how are these gifts recognized? How are these people chosen to use their gifts in worship? When and what may they perform? How should the congregation be encouraged to respond? These questions confront every leader of worship. On the one hand, we want people to share their gifts. On the other, we want to offer a unified service that engages the entire congregation in worship.

I've wrestled with these questions often over my years of music ministry. Many times after inviting someone to offer special music, I've had occasion to smile broadly in approval. Occasionally, I've moved into the shadows in embarrassment.

Here are some insights I've gained as I've striven to use people's gifts in worship. Although I will focus my attention on the ministry of special music, these principles apply to dramas, readings, or any special contribution to worship.

An Appropriate Performer

A beautiful voice is not the only prerequisite to being selected to sing a special number. Appropriate ability must be combined with a gracious spirit, a life of faith generally recognized as above public reproach, a strong sense of integrity, and a dedication to the task that seeks no personal gain.

How much ability is required? Some people draw attention to themselves because their abilities are painfully underdeveloped. Others try to impress you with their technical expertise. The people we seek in worship are those whose abilities don't get in the way of worship, who don't have to impress you with their abilities, as capable as they may be.

Somebody once asked a world-renowned singer how many lessons were required to become a good singer. The reply was, "Enough so that you can forget about them." The outward display of technique or the obvious lack of talent both have their liabilities.

So, how do we determine where people can best serve? In two words: prudently and patiently. I do not like to turn a captive audience over to soloists or Christian artists whom I have not observed in private and in different public settings.

Consequently, I feel most comfortable choosing people from our own adult Chancel Choir to perform special music. They are people who are "paying their dues," supporting the music ministry week in and week out. I also have observed them in a variety of settings and can sense something of the musical and spiritual respect that others have for them.

Yet not all gifted soloists have the time or freedom to sing in the choir. With these people, I find it helpful to spend fifteen to twenty minutes in a private interview and audition. During that time I gather some impressions and learn about the person's musical and spiritual background.

There can be a good deal of awkwardness when an individual's style is not in keeping with our style of worship and public performance. So, generally it is a safer policy to allow a new musician in our church sufficient time to get to know us.

Sometimes I give a new musician a smaller or more informal venue in which to minister so that I can see what kind of response he or she might engender. Such settings include an informal hymn sing, an adult fellowship class, a social occasion, or an evening of song at a summer family camp or conference.

I recall first meeting a young man in our church who said he was interested in arranging music, especially for instruments. We agreed on one or two projects for small ensembles, and his talent became readily evident. Over a period of six months, I found him a capable arranger and a talented keyboard accompanist, familiar with the intricacies of electronic keyboards and synthesizers. Not only has our friendship grown, but I've also been able to give him more exposure as my confidence in him has grown with each project we shared.

I also have discovered it helps to know which musical styles musicians, especially solo singers, feel most comfortable with. Some prefer the more classical oratorio, cantata, or art song; some have their roots in the gospel hymns of previous decades; others feel at home with the more rhythmic and personal interpretations of contemporary songs and ballads.

Choosing appropriate performers also means deciding how often to use people from outside the church, especially the Christian artists who crisscross the country performing their concerts. In a church like ours, we receive five to eight calls per week from performers wanting to sing in this church. From time to time, we do bring in guest artists in music or drama, and we host groups from

Christian colleges as a way of helping our people learn more about Christian higher education.

However, my philosophy as minister of music precludes administering a program filled with too much outside talent. For me it is vital that musically talented people within our own congregation have a chance to minister to their families and friends. In a church blessed with children's choirs, handbells, youth singers, orchestra, ensembles, and soloists, I feel the development of these gifts within our church — and the privilege of leading in worship those who know and love them — should be our first priority. In some cases, a sincere but somewhat unpolished performance by people who are "ours" is more conducive to worship than a slick presentation from an outside performer.

An Appropriate Message

We prefer a well-integrated worship service, in both music and text. To propel a particular theme in worship, I find it most helpful to choose various songs and musical selections for performance. Because of that, I need soloists who have sufficient flexibility and humility to accept an assignment. It also means I need to know who among our possible soloists might be able to sing a particular song most appropriately.

At our last missions-emphasis month, we were focusing on "The World at Our Doorstep," trying to catch a fresh glimpse of the internationals God was bringing to our community as well as the needy and underprivileged who live within a few miles of the church. While searching for suitable music, I came across the song "Lonely Voices Crying in the City" by Billie Hanks, Jr.

Musically, the song was simple, with a range of just a few notes. But its message was exactly right. So, I called one of our soloists and arranged to practice it for the service. We worked through the song, deciding where we would like to add interpretation, repetitions, interludes, and dynamics. The placement of that textual message in the service, combined with the artistic rendering of that simple song, made us more sensitive to the plight of immigrants and the homeless.

However, since it is impossible for one music minister to be aware of all the potential solo repertoire, it is good to give some freedom of choice to musicians. In other words, at times I choose the singer first, picking someone, perhaps, who has not had occasion to sing for some time. I will ask that person to select three or four songs that speak to the theme we're highlighting. Then we discuss the songs together and agree upon a selection. This dialogue gives the singer a chance to work within a known and familiar repertoire, and perhaps to introduce me to some new music. And it gives me occasion to maintain the focus of the service.

An Appropriate Style

After years in music ministry, I've found that what makes special music special is the way it's handled and prepared. Musical artistry is not just in *what* you sing or play, but *how* you present it. There can be unusual beauty in a simple folk song accompanied by guitar, or a lovely hymn sung by a dedicated, sensitive singer, or a five-part polyphonic motet. Each one, in its place, performed with care and craft, becomes an artistic experience. This continues to be one of the greatest challenges in church music — not only to perform the masterworks with authenticity and integrity, but also to choose and present the simple song or the prayerful response in just the right way.

One Good Friday, I conducted the Brahm's *Requiem* at First Evangelical Free Church. We had come to the end of Communion and had said the closing prayer but hadn't added the "Amen." In a sense the prayer never ended. The cellos started on that low F, and the music itself became a continuation of the prayer, a great unfolding of truth.

I remember coming to the part where we hear the shout, "Death, where is thy sting?" when Brahms sounds high strong chords so full of anticipation that we're all waiting, wondering, *What does death have to say now?*

There's no answer. The grave is silent. Christ has won the victory!

Then out of this silence comes the grand fugue, "Lord, thou art worthy!"

Not only the content but also the mood of the piece matched the service perfectly.

Another time we celebrated the Resurrection using a jazz piece with a rock beat from the musical *Celebrate Life*. We had people stream into the aisles, shouting to one another with the exhilaration of that throbbing beat: "He is alive! He is alive!"

At times the worship moment requires solemn contemplation, at others a gentle expression of joy. It's a matter of picking the right tool for the job, the right style for the right moment.

An Appropriate Response

How worshipers respond to the performance of a group, a choir, or a soloist can either enhance, hinder, or, yes, even destroy the spirit of worship. I'm referring not to what people do with the truth they've heard, but to their immediate response to the special music itself.

Sometimes applause is appropriate in worship, especially as an expression of praise, affirmation, or celebration. I look back with some amusement on the great Southern California Billy Graham Crusade in Anaheim Stadium in 1985. When Graham gave the familiar invitation to come forward, from various places in the stands would come sporadic bursts of applause. He repeatedly asked people not to do that. But it didn't stifle the joy and delight of some of the ethnic groups at seeing one of their own step out to accept Christ. That applause became one of the celebrative trademarks of those meetings.

After our orchestra and choir have sung and played a piece with a loud and dramatic ending, people frequently seem to want to do something to identify with it. There is nothing wrong with that kind of conclusion to a musical presentation, but it elicits a response — applause — that some would say is inappropriate. Yet is it always inappropriate or contrary or sinful? Applause could be yet another way of saying "Amen," "Yes, I agree," "Me, too."

By the same token, we have all sat in a place of worship or concert or recital hall when we felt that silence was the much better response. Someone has said that silence, even more than music, is the best way to express the inexpressible. Who has not cringed when, after a particularly powerful song, the moment has been shattered by unthinking, insensitive applause?

It is possible, however, to subtly prevent people from clapping if we feel applause would be counterproductive. For instance, when a soloist comes to the last note of her piece, she can remain intent, in effect holding the bubble in her hand, not releasing it, even after the last note has died away.

A thoughtful worship leader looks ahead and discerns the dramatic moments of the service and plans for an appropriate response. One Sunday our orchestra, choir, and congregation rendered a powerful, almost symphonic, setting of the hymn "Holy, Holy, Holy," arranged by Bob Walters. The orchestral instruments and full choral part of the grand climax beautifully amplifies the text: "God in three persons, blessed Trinity." It rises to new heights in a choral coda with three dramatic restatements of the word, *Holy*.

We foresaw the applause that would naturally follow, but thought silence would be a more meaningful response. So I told our organist, "The moment we finish the cutoff, I'd like you immediately to take the softest stop you have and play just the melody notes and perhaps the simplest transparent harmonies of "God in three persons. . . ."

That was all it took to be transported from the dynamic of full orchestra, choir, and pipe organ to the slightest whisper from the organ pipes. But it was enough to capture a completely contrasting side to the theme of that great hymn and help us meditate quietly upon it.

As the sounds of the organ slipped away, I stood at the pulpit, not releasing the congregation to sit down, and quietly said, "Worshipers are silent in the presence of a holy God; take and use this quiet, personal moment to adore." No words, no music, for thirty seconds!

Yes, applause may occur spontaneously or even haphazardly, but we can do our part to allow it or to inhibit it for a reason — to enhance the spirit of worship.

At their best, special music and other special contributions to worship are sacrifices to God. We are the performers, the actors, the prompters on the platform; God is the audience. *Soli Deo Gloria!*

Special music, then, is done on behalf of the congregation, leading them to send their thoughts and praises to God. That's what makes the offering special, and that's why we need to take care that it is done well.

We teach the Word and we sing praises; we sing both choruses and hymns; we sometimes pray with heads bowed and other times with faces up; we pray for each other privately and in small groups; we praise with voice and hands and, on rare occasions, have even danced! In short, we aim to worship not only with our minds, but also with our hearts.

— Jack Hayford

CHAPTER EIGHT
Engaging the Whole Person

During the opening of the last Olympics, everyone in the stadium joined hands and sang. On television talk shows, the guests greet one another and the host with smiles and handshakes or kisses. Athletes give each other high fives or dance in the end zone.

We're a far more expressive society than thirty years ago when I began ministry. Along the way, many churches have become more expressive, as well. More people seek worship that allows them to display more openly their joy and praise. It's not that they have a diminishing respect for the mind. They simply have an increasing need to experience their faith emotionally, and they see that the Bible enjoins such freedom.

In our ministry at Church on the Way, we've tried to offer worship that engages the whole person. We teach the Word and we sing praises; we sing both choruses and hymns; we sometimes pray with heads bowed and other times with faces up; we pray for each other privately and in small groups; we praise with voice and hands and, on rare occasions, have even danced! In short, we aim to worship not only with our minds, but also with our hearts.

The Value of Expressive Worship

Not everyone, of course, is comfortable with open expression of emotion in worship. Some are concerned emotional display will lead to unseemly behavior. Others believe that expressive worship is unworthy of thoughtful Christians.

We've tried to address those concerns while focusing on the value of worship that includes both head and heart. Let me, then, lay out a few reasons we feel a service must have not only firm intellectual content, but also a sensitive emotional element. Certainly, the Bible (the Psalms especially) shows that worship engages deep emotions. And countless individuals testify that expressive worship dramatically nurtures their faith. Yet, there are also strategic reasons for fashioning expressive worship.

● *It challenges the culture.* Even though our society is expressing emotions more openly, the legacy of the Enlightenment remains entrenched in many quarters. Western culture tends to value empirical analysis. We put life over a Bunsen burner, sort its colors of the spectrum, dissect it in a laboratory, break down its chemical components.

Rationality is a gift of God, and the church has gained immeasurably by the advances of the Enlightenment. But in some respects we've become subverted by it. Our culture sometimes tempts us to leave the heart behind. Sometimes we're fearful that our faith and worship won't be intellectually respectable. When rationality becomes the litmus test of the church's life, the life of the Spirit suffers. The spiritual life may not be purely emotional, but surely it is a combination of mind and heart.

Worship challenges this aspect of our culture. It subtly points out the insufficiency of pure rationality by pointing to the transcendence and inscrutability of God. Expressive worship highlights the intensity and joy of being committed in both mind and heart. It's one way to witness to the world about the new, full life that Christ offers.

● *It nurtures humility.* Many times our emotional reserve is but a fearful quest to retain control of our lives. We're especially afraid that if we surrender emotional control, we'll end up blithering idiots. God never makes fools of people, but he does expect us to give up the reigns of our lives to him. Expressive worship cultivates a willingness to be taught by and submit to the Holy Spirit.

A gifted artist and well-known actor (who performed both Shakespeare and a successful television series) attended our church several years ago. In his middle sixties, he was a man of fine taste, well-read, sophisticated. Although he'd become a Christian elsewhere, he decided to attend our church. He was impressed, he later told me, with the expressive quality of our congregation, noting especially the "childlikeness" our worship nutures in those who attend.

Naturally, we're not interested in destroying a person's individuality. But we do want people to die to self-will. We want them to release their pride and remain flexible in the Spirit. Expressive worship, because it nurtures the emotions, is one way to do that. It prevents spiritual arthritis (or, worse, rigor mortis!) in the body of Christ.

● *It creates a climate of warmth and acceptance.* When you develop an expressive atmosphere, you cultivate the spirit of fellowship, which creates a climate for evangelism.

Bernie was a successful accountant whose wife attended church regularly. He liked to hear the sermons, but he avoided the other, more expressive parts of worship. He would ask his wife to save him a seat, and thirty minutes into the service, as the sermon would begin, he would slip in.

One day he reluctantly agreed to attend the entire service with his wife. "I'll go with you," he warned her, "but only if we can sit so that I'm on the aisle and you're next to me. I don't want to hold hands with anybody but you." She agreed, and they went.

As soon as he sat down, however, the ushers, who saw the sanctuary filling rapidly, began placing folding chairs in the aisle at the end of the pews. My oldest daughter, a teenager at the time, sat next to him, unaware of Bernie's reserve. When a time came to join hands and raise them in praise, my five-foot-small daughter warmly and spontaneously grabbed Bernie's hand and raised it.

That was a turning point for Bernie. Although already a Christian, from that moment, he says, he became increasingly alive spiritually.

"She was just a little, teenage girl," he later said, "obviously so sincere, not trying to push me. I was simply drawn into the service."

• *It fosters commitment.* Rather than encouraging people to be placid observers, passing judgment on what is said and done, expressive worship demands participation and, therefore, commitment. In our service, people are sometimes asked to hold up their hands or move into small groups or greet one another. You cannot remain passive in our worship, and that fact spills over into the life of the church.

The Four Dimensions of Expressive Worship

In our services, we encourage people to do four things in worship, each of which helps engage the whole person.

1. Personalize their praise. Worship leaders help people praise God for his great gifts, like creation and salvation. But sometimes even devout Christians have a hard time grasping the immensity of these magnificent gifts. Praise then becomes a mere verbal recitation of theological truths.

Yet, if we can encourage people to personalize their praise, their worship will be more meaningful and their praise more heartfelt.

For instance, after I lead a praise chorus or hymn, I might say,

"We've just exalted Jesus' name in praise. Now let's praise God for something particular."

Then I'll use a teaching device to help people become specific. In one recent service, I held up my hand, pointed to one of my fingers, and said, "Do you know that a doctor can't tell you why you can move that finger. He can tell you the muscles and nerves that make it move, but he cannot explain fully why, when you decide to move a finger, you move it. Besides thanking God for the marvel of your physical creation, take your four fingers, and for each one think of a reason to praise God."

Then I'll illustrate what I mean. "My four are Becky, Jack, Mark, and Christy — my children. Maybe you'll name your kids, or perhaps your job. But list four things you are thankful for today."

This takes no more than thirty seconds, but immediately people begin thinking individually about how God has been good to them. Their praise of God becomes more personal and moving at that point.

After we've taught something new to our people, a new chorus for example, I'll personalize it with a jesting remark like this: "You were gracious to learn it with me, but just between you and me, let's admit it; that was hardly 'praise.' We were rehearsing, self-conscious about remembering the words. Fortunately, God wasn't listening to our rehearsal, but this time while you sing, he is! So this time let's let the words express our thanks to him."

I'll often sense a change in the room after I do something like that. We've gone from an adventure in learning to praising God in a fresh and personal way.

2. Verbalize their thoughts. To think and silently praise God is one thing, to express those thoughts in words another. It's the difference between knowing I love my wife and telling her. Telling her not only affirms her, it reinforces and deepens my love for her.

So, early in the service we help people talk. The easiest way to do that is by greeting them with, "Good morning!" to which they respond in kind. After an opening hymn or prayer of praise, we might encourage people to say, "Thank you, God" or "Amen!" in unison. Such suggestions hardly threaten or move people. At first, though, I'm not trying to get them to experience something meaningful as much as I am letting them hear the sound of their voices in worship.

At some point near the beginning, I also will have people greet one another. More particularly, I will give them something specific to say to people near them.

For example, recently I said, "This morning I was thinking of the verse, 'The Lord will perfect that which concerns me.' That verse has strengthened my life many times. This morning as you greet the person next to you, tell him or her about a verse that's meant something to you."

Knowing that some people won't be able to come up with a verse, I'll say, "If you're like me, when somebody tells me to think of a verse, I can't think of one. If that's your case, why not use mine this morning: 'The Lord will perfect what concerns me.' While we greet each other this morning, give your name, and then say your verse or assert with me, 'The Lord *will* perfect what concerns me.' "

3. Mobilize their bodies. Saying "I love you" to my wife may be better than just thinking it, but it is better still — more emotionally engaging for both of us — if I express that tangibly, with a hug or a kiss. Likewise, engaging the emotions in worship means engaging people's bodies.

The simplest way to do that is to get people to use their hands and arms. People can open their hands, facing palms upward with arms extended in front of them — a simple symbol of openness to receive God's blessing. At another time, their arms may be lifted up in adoration.

The point is to get them to express their praise in some physical way. The liturgical churches (which encourage kneeling and crossing oneself, for example) have appreciated for centuries the value of movement in worship. Our forms may be different, but not the substance of their meaning.

4. Love one another. We gather not as individuals praising God, but as a community. Corporate worship better engages emotions when people recognize one another's presence and, in some way, reach out to one another.

That can be fostered in subtle ways. Using easily memorized choruses or projecting hymn words on a screen helps. Such devices keep people's eyes up, looking around. Also, stepping off the platform from time to time and leading worship from the floor engenders a sense of community.

But there are more direct ways of involving people with one another. Toward the middle of the service, during a five minute segment we call "ministry time," we ask people to break into groups of four or five, with two or three people in a one row, for instance, turning around to join with people behind them. They talk, share requests and concerns, and then pray.

It continually amazes me what happens during this time. If we have two thousand people in a service, a couple hundred will be wiping their eyes by the end of the prayer time.

Naturally, this opportunity threatens some people, but this threat also attracts them. Many people say the first eight or ten times they came to our church, they didn't know why they came. They "hated" the prayer circles. As the time approached, their hands would sweat, and during the time, they simply listened and watched, letting others talk and pray. But slowly they became involved and touched by these times, so much so they join the church because of them.

I believe people willingly persevere through their initial discomfort because they yearn to be heard and loved. Ministry time is a brief but moving opportunity to let them be loved in corporate worship.

Begetting a Response

Although people want freedom to express themselves emotionally in worship, they often find it intimidating to do so. In order to ease their discomfort and encourage greater participation, we keep in mind a number things as we prepare and lead our services.

● *Remember your purpose.* I believe God wants us to engage our emotions in worship, but not for their own sake. It would be unworthy to aim for a mere psychological effect. So we don't do anything in worship unless it has a firm biblical base. That doesn't mean I need a proof text for counting praise on my four fingers, but it does mean I want my exercises to lead people to something biblical, like praising God.

Careful planning helps keep the purpose focused. The exercises I use to lead people to personalize or verbalize praise, for example, are carefully thought out ahead of time. When I first began ministry, I would write them out word for word. Now I simply think them through carefully.

I will note specific types of people who will be at the service — married couples, widows, teenagers, single mothers, and others. I will think especially about people who might resist expressive worship. I then will craft my remarks so that everyone will be graciously encouraged to participate, and participate fully in the worship of God.

- *Explain the biblical background of the unusual.* People will be inclined to participate in a new worship experience if they see its biblical rationale.

Why, for example, should anybody even consider dance in worship, even a simple back-and-forth step? It's likely to embarrass or put people off. But if they see biblical grounds for rejoicing in this way, they'll be more likely to participate.

So, I will cite a verse or two from the Psalms or mention David's dance before the Lord as I invite people to learn a simple dance of praise. After that I might add, "I've got to tell you that this word *dance* gives me problems; it seems a little foolish. But, here it is right in the Bible. Why didn't God put that in The Book of Mormon or some place I wouldn't have to believe?"

People will laugh, and the tension is released, because they've been anxious about it. I'll continue, "But here it says 'Dance,' and I don't think the Lord wants to make fools of us. So why don't we join in." I rarely lead a simple dance of joyous worship, but when I have, people offer a whole, healthy response.

- *Include everyone, but give people a gracious way to respond.* If you're going to lead an expressive form of worship, everyone must be invited to participate. To tell people "Don't join in if you don't feel like it" is to consign expressive worship to the more exuberant.

Instead, expressive worship should be seen as normal, as something everybody can participate in regardless of temperament.

When I invite people to participate, I assume everybody will join in. At the same time, I recognize people's fear and awkwardness. So I still ask everyone to participate, but I give them a way to feel comfortable doing so.

During ministry time I might say, "We're going to join together in small circles now. If you've never done this before, we understand this can be too much and too quick. We want you to feel comfortable; we wouldn't embarrass you for the world. But we've also learned that it's more embarrassing to do nothing than to get in a circle! So accept the invitation to join a circle of prayer. Feel free to say, 'I've never done this before. Could I just watch?' But even if you just watch, join the circle. You'll love it, and those with you will love you!"

In this way, people experience expressive worship and yet at their own pace.

● *Acknowledge their fears.* People are anxious about trying new things, especially in a group. But I've found that acknowledging these normal anxieties goes a long way toward relieving them.

Before a moment of simultaneous praise, in which we encourage people to speak their praises with voices at conversational level, I also might say, "When we lift our voices today and praise the Lord, we're not asking you to scream, holler, or shriek. In fact, if you do shriek, you may find an usher or elder immediately telling you to stop." People usually chuckle at that, because that's what some of them have been wondering. Once it's acknowledged, people are relieved: *Well, maybe I can do this if I'm not going to have to tolerate somebody going berserk.*

● *Soften self-consciousness.* Most people are self-conscious when they participate in something new. Anything a worship leader can do to lessen that will enhance the experience for people.

That's one reason evangelists play music as people come forward for a decision. It's not music to get people in the mood for conversion. Rather, many people aren't going to walk down the aisle to the clop, clop, clop of their footsteps reverberating through the room. Music softens that sound and removes one unnecessary barrier.

Likewise, people feel more free to speak if the sound of their voice isn't the only thing they hear. So when we ask people to greet one another or share during ministry time, we have our instrumentalists play softly in the background.

● *Lead people verbally.* The moment after you've invited people to respond can be awkward. That lapse of silence puts undue pressure on people. Most people hesitate to be the first to greet or raise hands or join a prayer group, so everyone waits for someone else to begin.

During the greeting time, I might say, "There are two or three people around you. Greet them." And to get people started, I might add lightheartedly, "You can move. You're not fastened to the floor." Moving toward the congregation, I might laugh and gesture with open hands, "Go ahead. That's right." And I'll keep talking and encouraging as people move and the room begins to buzz.

Leading verbally provides a bridge for people that eases them into the experience.

● *Don't overwhelm people with the new.* We usually begin the service with something familiar, perhaps with a hymn like "All Hail the Power of Jesus' Name" or "Holy, Holy, Holy." And whenever we stretch people to experience a new dimension of worship, we immediately come back to something they're familiar with. So after leading people in a new song where I've had them join hands, I will ask them to release their hands and sing some old standard. People enjoy new expressions of worship more if the service contains elements they already are comfortable with.

● *Touch a variety of emotions.* We help people experience fuller worship if we aim for a variety of emotions. That's easiest to see and do in the selection of music.

With choruses the thought is succinct, the melody simple, and the ability of people to relax and praise God with affection is enhanced. In classic hymns, like "Immortal, Invisible," the progression of thought through the verses, the doctrinal content, and the dignity of the music requires more effort to sing, but it also encourages adoration at a another level.

Naturally, some people are more comfortable with some forms of emotion than others. Which emotion is touched is less important than that emotion is engaged in the worship of God.

- *Treat people with respect.* I believe most people come to worship because they care about the Lord, and they want to show him they care. So I shape my remarks to reflect that. I don't aim a cannon at them because they're not consecrated enough. Instead, I affirm their presence and build on the faith that their presence indicates.

This is especially important if I want to lead people into expressive worship. Haranguing them for their inhibitions will only make them more hesitant.

Treating people with respect means, first of all, *inviting* people to join in some new aspect of worship. As I ask people to participate in a moment of simultaneous yet quiet verbal praise, I might say, "You may never have done this before, and I understand that God's not going to unlove you if you don't do it today. But do join in. It is a wonderful and scriptural way to express thanks to God."

Respecting people also means acknowledging them after they've tried something new, especially if it's been awkward for some. After one of those times I've led people in a simple dance of childlike praise, I might say, "That was gracious of you to do that. I know it was awkward for some of you, but I appreciate your willingness to join in."

Whole Worship Touches the Whole Person

One of our members and his friend from another large congregation visited each other's church together. Afterwards, our member told me about his friend's reaction.

"My friend says that the difference between the services was that at his church the service *speaks* to you, but here the service speaks to *you*," emphasizing the personal impact.

As far as that is true, I believe it's due to the more expressive nature of our service. People aren't there only for intellectual exercise, or as observers. They do participate with their minds, but also with their emotions.

It's no wonder, then, that they feel personally addressed in the service. Their whole person has been involved.

Part Three
Changes

___

In responding to God, we should be open to using every expression of beauty and genius, which are reflections of his own nature.

— *Howard Stevenson*

CHAPTER NINE

Adding Creativity without Losing the Congregation

When I came to First Evangelical Free Church, the congregation began every service by singing the first verse of "All Hail the Power of Jesus' Name." Shortly after I joined the staff, I asked and received permission from Pastor Swindoll to change our opening hymn.

It wasn't long, however, before I began getting notes written on bulletins asking me why we didn't sing "Coronation" (often misspelled "Coronashun" or "Cornations"). Although I can see humor in the situation now, at the time I felt threatened. I didn't know how widespread the objections were.

The experience pointed up the uneasiness, even fear, people often feel about change in their patterns of worship. We all love progress, but we're reluctant when change is imposed upon us!

"You would think that of all places, all communities, it would be in the church where we would most welcome the creativity and freshness and adventure of new things," says Eugene Peterson in *Running with the Horses*. "But instead that's the very place we are most threatened."

Why Change Isn't Always Welcome

Why do people resist change, especially in church? Habit and heritage are two big reasons. We all like to settle back in the old chair, even though there might be a broken spring or two; it's where we feel most at ease. And we all have notions about what worship should be. Often the ideas remain from childhood. Frankly, most of us are as defensive in our Christianity as in any other area of our lives. When someone suggests changes in the worship service, the common response is akin to the apocryphal seven last words of the church: "We've never done it that way before."

People who invoke the seven last words sometimes have a point. Worship leaders should be like baseball umpires: the more unnoticed they are, the better the job they are doing. C. S. Lewis wrote, "The perfect church service would be one we were almost unaware of: our attention would have been on God." We dare not let the means of worship intrude on the experience of the sacred.

People also especially treasure the music of their formative years, whether the popular music of their youth or the worship patterns of their most formative years spiritually. It's these experiences of the sacred that indelibly stamp themselves on people's minds and create worship memories that we tamper with at our peril. People often voice their strongest feelings over worship music; it touches their roots, their emotions.

I've talked to many church leaders about adding creativity to worship, and they say, "But the people in my congregation come from an old German Baptist background . . ." or "Ours is a little farming community, and if we were to do anything like what's been suggested, they'd hang me from the nearest limb!"

As worship leaders, we have to recognize that creativity poses a threat. Daring to try new things always carries a risk. I like the two Oriental characters for the word *crisis*. In both Japanese and Chinese, they mean "threatening opportunity." That's how I view the challenge of using creativity to bring the worship experience to people in new and refreshing ways.

Why Creativity Is Worth the Risk

I believe creativity in worship is indispensable, in spite of the dangers. Worship is a verb, as author Robert Webber reminds us, a response to God, and it requires active participation. In responding to God, I believe we should be open to using every expression of beauty and genius, which are reflections of his own nature. Whether the "Hallelujah" chorus or "Worthy Is the Lamb," prayer or Scripture, testimony or proclamation, the elements of worship —creatively employed in praise of God — give us yet another glimpse of the face of God.

Worship is a relational response. In some ways it's like marriage. I've been married to my wife, Marilyn, for more than thirty-six years. The more routine and predictable we allow our marriage to become, the more we begin to take our relationship for granted. But if every morning we share together some new expression, gift, act of love, or experience, our relationship will keep growing.

Similarly, when worship becomes predictable, it can become ordinary and lose its impact. By using creativity in challenging yet nonthreatening ways, worship can enliven people's relationship with God. Most Christians want to remain open to every part of God's person; creative worship helps them sustain their hunger to know God more deeply.

How to Do It Wisely

How do we move away from stiff, inflexible, and colorless worship? How do we utilize creativity to help people live, again as Eugene Peterson described, "zestfully, exploring every experience, pain and joy, enigma and insight, fulfillment and frustration as a dimension of human freedom, searching through each for sense and grace"? How do we add such creativity to worship without turning people off?

1. Stay within the boundaries of trust. Worship leaders need the trust of the people to whom they are ministering. Our congregation has come to know our style of worship. Although we're always looking for fresh ways of approaching worship, we work with components people are used to and in ways that will not shock them.

The church, after all, is a community of faith. Creativity should enhance, rather than disrupt, that community. It should underscore the feeling that we are all here to share the love and grace of Christ, and that there is more that binds us than divides us.

One boundary is the congregation's sense of dignity. This may be different from church to church, but all congregations have a point beyond which it is unwise to go. Determining that point comes from intuition and careful experimentation. Once people know we respect their sense of dignity, they will move with us into the unknown, daring to risk even the unusual.

One recent Sunday our Chancel Choir sang and clapped a special rhythm to Allen Pote's anthem, "Clap Your Hands and Sing." When we finished with a strong, exciting conclusion, I invited the congregation to give a "clap offering" to God as an expression of joy and praise, and they did with pleasure.

Then, one of our associate pastors came to the platform and surprised me with the suggestion that the entire congregation learn, right then and there, the clapping rhythm of the anthem. Then, as he mentioned items of thanks and praise, everyone, under my direction, clapped for joy to the Lord.

Risky? Different? Daring? Yes. This experiment was outside our usual boundaries, but still within the bounds of our congregation's sense of dignity. Because we had demonstrated over the years that we would stay within those boundaries, the congregation enthusiastically participated.

Another boundary I call the "quantity quotient." People can take only so much newness. Too much is an overload. We must operate in their comfort zone, even as we push the border of that zone further and further out. I never plan more than one unusual worship expression per service. And I always give people permission not to participate, although that very permission usually helps them feel comfortable about participating.

2. Mix the old with the new. Whenever we introduce something new, it's good to come back to something familiar. Even great choral masterworks, although traditional, will challenge the listening tastes of many of our people. So I will balance such a presentation with choral offerings that most of our people appreciate more naturally. In the same way, a highly contemporary musical will need to be counterbalanced with a familiar solo or hymn.

3. Don't manipulate. Creativity can effectively engage people with the genuine emotion of the gospel. But we should not use emotion to manipulate. The object isn't to create euphoria or bring tears. Nor should creativity be employed for shock value. Rather, it should fill worship with an air of spontaneity, freshness, and adventure in responding to God.

Emotion isn't an end in itself. It is a by-product of genuine worship. I was once at a worship service in which the leaders began by telling us to clap and move with the music. They hadn't led us to experience joy or celebration; they just wanted us to express the emotions. Instead of being a means of expressing joy, the techniques seemed to be their means of trying to produce joy. I felt manipulated. People are happy to respond when they've been given something substantive to respond to and an appropriate way to express their response.

Most people will resent it if they sense we have used a moment inappropriately, and they will be especially sensitive to innovations at intense moments in worship. So I don't use those moments to get them to do something they would otherwise resist, like clapping or raising their hands. If I want to introduce such elements, I must find ways to prepare people for them. It's best to leave alone the intense moments of worship until people have accepted the innovations I've introduced at other times in the service.

By the way, creative worship isn't always focused on emotion. Worship uses the whole range of human responses, from the highly rational to the highly emotional, and many things between.

A good worship leader utilizes it all.

4. *Remain sensitive to people's response.* Then there are times when we try something new and it doesn't quite come off. For example, our "Praise in Motion" group, a ministry using modest dance and body movement, has met some resistance when we've included it in worship. Although some people loved it (I personally am a great fan), we backed off for a while. We worship leaders need to be sensitive to how creativity is applied. We want people to remain open to innovation in worship.

Because creativity in worship is a high-risk endeavor, we must be especially sensitive to how people accept even the smallest changes. Before and after every innovation, I ask these questions:

— Does this heighten "spectatorism," or will it involve people in worship in new and meaningful ways?

— Is there a danger of fostering a "Can you top this?" syndrome with this worship experiment?

— Does this take people too far out of their comfort zone?

— Is this innovation an acceptable risk? If it bombs, can we recover gracefully?

5. *Get affirmation of colleagues.* In developing and implementing creative worship, it helps to have the affirmation of colleagues. This is crucial, of course, if you work with a multiple staff. At First Evangelical Free Church, I am close to our pastoral staff, and they help me face that adventure. They must feel included in the new things we do in worship.

But even solo pastors know key people both inside and outside the church they can consult with new worship ideas. Such people can give suggestions, and they can wave red flags at the occasional bad idea. (It does happen!) And, heaven forbid, if things should go wrong, insiders who have endorsed the idea can take some of the heat.

Above all, I remind myself to be patient with creative worship innovations. Good ideas don't need to be implemented immediately; they will still be good ideas in six months or a year. We need to lay the proper groundwork, think them through carefully, and get all the advice we can. Chances of improving worship through creativity will rise dramatically with careful preparation on all fronts.

Putting Creativity to Work

Creativity is more than changing the Scripture and responsive readings or the numbers of the hymns. As I mentioned in an earlier chapter, a working axiom of mine for worship is: "The lower the predictability, the higher the impact." And there are many ways to achieve that.

Lessening the distinction between the platform and the people is a good place to start. Sometimes we begin worship with quiet choruses and no visible leadership — an empty pulpit. I remain seated on the pastor's bench and simply lead out with my voice, with the choir supporting me from behind. Something like that suggests we are waiting upon God in worship, without the interference of human personality.

Also, some areas of our worship center are not directly visible from the platform. So from time to time I take a hand microphone and seek the eyes of the people in those areas. Or I move a step or two down the platform to lower the sight lines a bit.

There are many ways to involve people in worship. Our asking children to come forward to sing, read, or pray brings adults to attention. Sometimes we arrange for as many as four or six people to stand in the congregation and read a declaration of God's goodness, majesty, or mercy. Another way is to give the congregation a simple but meaningful part to recite in a reading. For example, Psalm 136 has the recurring refrain, "For his lovingkindness endures forever," that people can recite.

I've also had the congregation join in by saying, "Alleluia! Alleluia!" at my signal as I've read the hymn text by Fred Pratt Green, a portion of which goes like this:

> When in our music God is glorified,
> and adoration leaves no room for pride,
> it is as though the whole creation cried,
> *Alleluia! Alleluia!*

How oft in making music we have found
a new dimension in the world of sound,
as worship moved us to a more profound
Alleluia! Alleluia!

And did not Jesus sing a song that night
when utmost evil strove against the light?
Then let us sing for whom he won the fight.
Alleluia! Alleluia!

Let every instrument be tuned for praise!
Let all rejoice who have a voice to raise!
And may God give us faith to sing always:
Alleluia! Alleluia!

Using fresh vocabulary can also inject some creativity into worship. Sometimes I desperately yearn to say something with a novel and expanded vocabulary. Books of poetry and creative prose help me do that (see the bibliography).

One Easter we read a paraphrased version of 1 Corinthians 15 from a book called *Epistles Now*. Someone began reading, "The high point, the constantly recurring theme and the grand climax and the great symphony of the gospel is the resurrection of Jesus Christ." The ideas are nothing new. We know what's being said, but we hear it in a fresh, delightful way.

We took a similar approach not long ago when Chuck spoke on "Changing Times and Changeless Truths." I used a topical Bible to create a Scripture mosaic from Psalm 11, 2 Timothy 2 and 3, Malachi 3, and Hebrews 13 (Living Bible) as a responsive reading.

Also, many responsive readings can be given to a readers' theater, a group of people who practice and present a reading.

In addition, one can use hymns as prayers, as many people have done with the Psalms. For example, "Immortal, Invisible," and "Be Thou My Vision," work well as prayers.

Even the sermon can be adapted in different ways. On occasions, we've divided the sermon into portions and then sung songs between them. Once the choir sang the Bach motet "Jesu, Priceless Treasure," which focuses on Romans 8, and we had five-minute sermons between the chorales that so powerfully stated the text.

On another occasion, two of our pastors preached a dialogue sermon on the person and character of Jesus Christ. Back and forth they spoke, one about Jesus as God, the other extolling Christ's humanity.

Once Chuck and I moved the sermon up a bit, to allow the congregation to respond in song for ten or fifteen minutes afterward.

The possibilities are nearly endless. The point is: put creativity to work.

The Worship Leader as Catalyst

Worship leaders are really catalysts. We help release something that is already in people. At my church I have a variety of means to do that — a choir, a pipe organ, people who can read interpretively, handbells, people who do signing.

But no matter what a church's resources or how creativity is applied, the aim remains constant: to help worshipers sense, in a new way, the majesty of God.

Even within the confines of a traditional service, and without adjusting the rubrics at all, we can introduce changes that can revitalize the tone and tenor of the service.

— *John Killinger*

CHAPTER TEN

Revitalizing Lethargic Liturgy

London theater audiences have been entranced for some time by Peter Shaffer's *Lettice and Lovage*, a comedy starring Maggie Smith. Smith plays the part of a guide in a rather unexciting National Trust home. Bored with the job, she begins spicing up her presentations with highly imaginative concoctions about the families that lived there and the royalty who visited them. One fanciful story involves Queen Elizabeth I, who is said to have tripped on the stairway and been caught in midair by her host, who was subsequently knighted for his deft act!

I couldn't help thinking, the day after seeing the play, what the woman played by Maggie Smith could do for some of the unimaginative worship services I've sat through or even led. She'd spark a one-woman liturgical renaissance.

Having only recently moved back to an academic setting after several years in the pastorate, I'm quite aware that we ministers are not that free to invent our material out of whole cloth or to introduce it without general consent among our congregations. There is, nevertheless, a great deal we can do to enliven the worship offered up on most Sundays by our parishioners.

For big changes, such as placing the offering after the sermon (where by both theology and tradition it properly ought to be, if I may say so), it is undoubtedly best to work through a worship committee and perhaps even obtain a mandate of the congregation. I've known pastors who shortened their tenure by acting presumptuously in shaping or reordering the liturgy, even though the congregation appeared to be largely apathetic about it before the "tampering" took place.

But even within the confines of a traditional service, and without adjusting the rubrics at all, we can introduce changes that can revitalize the tone and tenor of the service. To do so doesn't require taking the liberties assumed by the guide in *Lettice and Lovage*. It merely requires our thoughtful devotion to the details of the liturgy.

Prayers that Evidence Thought

Consider the prayers, which interlace the service, set a mood for the worshipers, and help move everything along from the time the congregation gathers until it is ready to be dispersed again into the world.

It's a temptation to regard prayers as mere conversational interludes during which we can voice whatever we happen to be feeling at the moment. It's not uncommon to stand and offer prayers that, genuine as they are, are filled with rather mindless thoughts and impressions spoken in the language of cliché.

I once heard a man complain of his minister's casual attitude toward praying. He said, "My wife even makes a list before she goes to the grocery store. You'd think anyone would have the decency to think through what he wanted to say to God!"

George A. Buttrick, the great New York preacher and chaplain to Harvard University, said on many occasions that if he had time before a service to prepare only the prayers or his sermon, he would choose every time to spend it on the prayers. He knew that accuracy of thought and phrasing, together with a prayerful spirit, brings a sense of reality to worship and helps bind worshipers to the Spirit of God.

Stanley Mooneyham, the former president of World Vision, called me once to say that he and his wife, Nancy, would like to visit our early worship service on a particular Sunday. Delighted to hear that, I asked Stan if he would offer the morning prayer for us. When he consented, I said, "Now, Stan, the early service is rather small. We have it in the chapel, and there won't be many people." I didn't want him to expect too much.

But the size of the crowd mattered not at all to Stan.

When he got up to pray, he spoke one of the most beautifully composed prayers I have ever heard. It was in several parts, each part concerned with a separate area of our praying, and one part flowed to another with the grace of a sonnet by Shakespeare or a composition by Mozart.

Afterward, people wanted copies of the prayer because it expressed so well what they wanted to say to God.

I'm convinced that if we considered more carefully what to say in our public prayers, the prayers alone would raise the spiritual temperature of our congregations by fifteen degrees. Whatever is worth saying publicly to God is worth premeditation.

Affirmations that Reflect Current Faith

Affirmations of faith? Deadly, most people think.

"I believe in God the Father Almighty . . ." Good theology, but heavy. And dull, when you repeat it Sunday after Sunday.

But suppose I rewrite the affirmation occasionally, substituting for the traditional language some thoughts for our times. Here's one from my book *Lost in Wonder, Love, and Praise: Prayers and Affir-*

mations for Christian Worship. I composed it for a Sunday in the springtime:

> *I believe in the beauty of spring that is known in windy skies, blossom-ing fruit trees, waving jonquils, and sweet-smelling grass.*
>
> *I believe in the warmth of a friendship that is communicated in gentle eyes, a loving smile, a fond touch of the hand, and an arm laid on the shoulder.*
>
> *I believe in the power of Christ, whose presence is felt in every season of the year but especially now, when life wells up everywhere and folks feel a quickening in their souls because it is spring and sum-mer is on the way.*
>
> *I believe Christ is responsible for both spring and friendship, and that the excitement I feel today is related to the fact that he was dead but is alive forevermore, not only in our memories but in the truest kind of actuality.*
>
> *I worship him by coming here, and say, "Hallelujah! Christ is alive and in this very place!"*

Affirmations need to affirm a faith that is current. While the ancient affirmations link us with the sound theology of the past, our new creations can tie that theology to the thought forms and con-cerns of the people in our pews. When our people can say, *Yes! That's what I believe!* we have helped enliven their worship.

Scripture Readings that Live

The reading of Scripture takes place in every church on Sun-day morning. It's a cut-and-dried event, too brief to worry much about in the overall planning of the service.

Or so goes the conventional wisdom.

I still haven't forgotten the confession of a layman in a church I attended years ago. "I get along very well in the worship service," he said, "until the preacher gets up to read the Bible. Then some-thing happens to me. It's like a curtain drops in my mind, and I shut off. I guess I'm just a contemporary man, and it's an ancient book, and I have a hard time listening to it."

There may not be a lot of those "contemporary" people out

there in my congregation, but I always worry about them. What if they shut off and miss the Word of the Lord?

How can we help people to listen to the Scripture reading? One way is by being sure it is read as clearly and winsomely as possible, so that the power of the words breaks through.

A few months ago, the actor Arthur Petersen was presenting his one-man show about Robert Frost, *Fire and Ice,* in our church's Commonwealth Theater. Impressed by Petersen's personal piety as well as his dramatic skills, I invited him to read from the Old and New Testaments at a morning worship service. It was a treat beyond anything I had imagined.

Familiar texts leapt to life, danced, turned, twisted, revealed aspects of themselves I had never seen, and then concluded like a graceful ballerina finishing her act and bowing low before the audience. No one breathed. We were torn between worship and applause. We had heard the Word!

As one untrained in drama, I probably shouldn't attempt to give dramatic readings of the Scriptures; that would be posturing, and it would call attention to the wrong things. But I can be better prepared to read than I sometimes am. One trick is to print the texts in orator type so I can see them easily; another is to familiarize myself with those texts so completely that I'm able to communicate them without excessive strain or fumbling.

I worshiped for several years with a church that used lay people to read the lections each Sunday, rotating them so that each person on a team of a dozen readers read only a few times a year. The readers were given simple instructions by a local speech professor and were coached individually when they sought assistance. The variety kept the readings interesting, and, perhaps more important, reminded us Sunday by Sunday that the Bible belongs to the people and is not the exclusive domain of the clergy.

In the desiderata department, I have always wished for a choral reading group in my church that frequently would read the Scriptures on Sunday morning. I have heard such groups occasionally at conferences and in college or university chapels and found them extraordinarily powerful. By alternating parts between soloists, small groups, and the entire choir, they are able to move almost instantly from a whisper to a shout, from music to cacophony, from thunder to moonlight, and the effect is spine-tingling.

No one yawns when the Scriptures are read with the skill they deserve.

Preaching that Captivates

The sermon is probably more exclusively the business of the preacher than any other part of the liturgy, and, because it normally requires more time than almost anything else, it offers us the greatest opportunity to invest the service with power and vitality. Granted that not many of us are stem-winders, what can we do to improve the contribution of the sermon to the worship as a whole?

I suggest we begin by thinking in terms of *renewsal*. No, not *renewal* but *renewsal:* getting the *news* back into preaching.

As I visit churches and ministers, I find some preachers tend, because of their great familiarity with the message of Christianity, to assume everybody in their congregations has heard the message. Therefore they bring little evangelistic fervor to their preaching and fall into the rut of what I call "footnote preaching," dealing with secondary concerns such as managing personal loneliness, coping with grief, and leading a moral life in an immoral society.

The latter are important, but they are important only after people have met Christ and decided to make him the center of their lives. If Christ is not exalted regularly in our sermons, they soon become moralistic homilies, not words to raise the dead.

Worse, congregations begin to think of themselves as sophisticated or uptown and actually start to deplore too much emphasis on Christ and the Spirit at work among them. They may even sneer at a new minister who talks too much about Jesus and not enough about the cultural trends or sociological musings they have been accustomed to hearing.

When this happens, churches die from a lack of spiritual oxygen. The only thing to save them is a renewal in preaching. We have to remember Who it is we preach about.

Delivery is also important. Even sermons focusing on Jesus

can be dull and routine unless I take care to make them otherwise. My experience of Christ must be continually fresh, and my expression of that experience faithful and effervescent, if my preaching is to be effective.

"Seeing" truth — perceiving it with the right side of the brain — is especially important. And, when we've learned to do this, we'll soon be seeing Christ everywhere — in books, plays, art galleries, newspapers, and all our personal encounters. Most good stewards of the mysteries of life keep a notebook or journal of their sightings, so that they can recollect them months and years afterward and then distill their essence into usable form — in the minister's case, into sermons.

Everywhere I go, I urge preachers to develop the habit of writing thoughts, observations, anecdotes, and experiences in notebooks; and, just as faithfully, I hear later from these preachers, "I'm so glad I began keeping a notebook. Now I never run out of preaching material. My sermons are fresher than they've been in years!"

Some ministers find that even varying the form of the sermon improves their communications skills. They cast their thoughts into dialogue sermons, dramatic monologues, sermonic epistles to particular persons or biblical characters, imaginary newscasts, story sermons, and even musical presentations.

The important thing, I've found, is to see the sermon in its true perspective. It is not a twenty-minute space in the liturgy merely to be filled with my talk. It is an opportunity within the orchestration of the divine service to speak for Christ in the most imaginative, communicative way possible, so that the Holy Spirit finds the situation combustible and can truly ignite the hearts of the congregation.

Music that Motivates

To this point, I've said nothing about music, although it doubtless plays one of the most critical roles in helping the congregation worship with enthusiasm. The reason I've waited is that in most instances it is the part of the service least under our control. Many musical directors or ministers of music have rather independent feelings about the choice and disposition of church music and tend to be somewhat jealous of their prerogatives.

But even in situations in which we have no direct control over the music, we often hold considerable power of negotiation within the framework of relationships and can make suggestions regarding the kind of musical selections that will best serve the purposes we envision.

I've served all kinds of churches, from small, country churches where the pianist couldn't play hymns with more than one flat or sharp, to large, city churches with fabulous organs and paid choir personnel. What I have learned about church music is that the majority of people in any congregation, whether in the country or the city, prefer music that is (1) singable by even the untalented people, (2) simply and memorably worded, (3) in English, and (4) charged with deep and true emotion.

I have two personal beefs about the music in most of the worship services I attend (including my own). One is that it is too heavily weighted by old hymns and classical anthems, giving the liturgy an air of mustiness and antiquity. The other is that the contemporary hymns and anthems are often poorly written and scored, so that they amount to what conductor Roger Shaw calls "holy slush."

The solution? Work. We have to dig out the best of contemporary music and retain the classic works of old. We have to plan the musical fare with the care we do our sermons or prayers. If it is true that more doctrine is learned from hymns than from sermons, and that Christianity sings, not speaks, its way in the world, then we should spare no effort to insure that the music with which we worship God is the finest music of our time.

A Tone that Invites

Finally, there is the matter of the tone of the service — its temper and personality — which is largely in our hands.

Is the service positive in its outlook? Then it is probably because we exude these characteristics. Is it predictable and plodding? Again, it is probably an extension of the worship leader's attitude.

Take a simple item like the announcements. They can be regarded as a necessary evil to be dispatched with as swift a nod as possible. Or, one may evidence no particular attitude toward them and merely muddle through them.

I prefer to look brightly upon announcements as an expression of the theology of Incarnation, and deliver them with a kind of lightness and happiness that reproduces such an atmosphere in the congregation. I suspect my people prefer to receive the announcements each Sunday in such a way.

Even the lowly benediction is significant for the way it continues and climaxes the mood of a good service. The easy way out is to intone a few words that I memorized years ago when I began ministry: "May the Lord bless you and keep you . . ." It can become mindless for both the benedictor and the benedictees.

I like the story of the young minister who spent so much time talking baby talk to the recent addition to his family that he lapsed one Sunday morning and said, "Now may gracey, mercy, and peacey . . ."

But, rather than some vapid verbalization, wouldn't it be richer and more meaningful for the congregation to be dismissed with a blessing that thoughtfully draws to a conclusion the service they have been offering to God that particular day, something that forms a natural bridge between the themes they actually have dealt with and the life they are going out to live in the world?

If the service has centered on the seasons of life, for example, why not a benediction that concludes:

Now may God, who has ordained the seasons of the year and the seasons of life as well, grant you serenity and joy in this season of your soul, and life everlasting in the world to come, through Jesus who died and lives forevermore. Amen.

Or if the service was a Communion service, why not words of parting that say:

Now may God, who has fed us at his table with the gift of his own Son, continue to feed us through this week on his Holy Spirit, that we may be led into every pathway intended for us and possess the joy that has been promised us, through Jesus Christ our Lord. Amen.

These aren't major changes of the structure of worship; they're minor alterations with major significance. If worshiping God is the greatest joy and privilege we have, and I believe it is, then we'll want to craft every service of worship like a great artist's masterpiece: grand and beautiful in conception, and faithful in the execution of even the smallest details.

PART FOUR

Special Audiences and Occasions

There is no part of our service in which the non-Christian visitor is not invited to participate fully. We want to nurture an atmosphere where people sense God's presence and respond to him.

— *Jack Hayford*

CHAPTER ELEVEN

Including Non-Christians in Christian Worship

In each Sunday morning congregation sit many for whom Jesus is not yet Lord. Whatever their reasons for attending, they have come more to observe than worship. Their presence presents worship leaders with a challenge: How can we involve non-Christians in a service in which the main act is the worship of Christ?

We could conform our worship to the tastes and expectations of the unbelieving visitor. While that might make non-Christians comfortable, it would reduce our worship to less than an expression of devotion, adoration, and commitment to God.

Our services at Church on the Way consist of three parts: ministry to the Lord, ministry to the saints, and ministry to the world. We minister to the Lord through our worship and praise. We minister to the saints — to each other — by sharing in fellowship, love, and prayer. Ministry to the world happens primarily through the week as our members minister in their daily lives, yet part of our service attempts to equip them for their ministries.

But we also minister to the world during our services by encouraging unbelievers who are present to participate in the service and to accept Christ by the end. So, we believe our worship service, although based on the Scriptures and aimed at Christian worship, can remain sensitive to unbelieving visitors.

Here are some things we try to do during each service to make the non-Christian feel a part of the service.

Make Them Comfortable

We recognize that many visitors find our worship service unusually open and expressive. Because they are on unfamiliar turf, we consciously try to make them feel comfortable. Here's how we do it.

● *Invite them to relax.* We do this before the service formally begins. I walk in and from floor level welcome them with an introduction like this: "Good morning, everyone! Isn't it a great day? Nice to see you. We're going to praise the Lord in just a few minutes, and as we do, I want us to let our hearts be filled with wonder and praise. Don't worry about making an impression; here it's okay to be yourself. We can't impress God with how smart or sophisticated we are anyway, can we? So let's come together as his children and let the joy of the Lord Jesus fill this house today. He's alive! He's risen! And we want to praise him! Do you feel that way?"

We've found that many people do feel that way, so they respond. Once they are given permission to relax, they often do.

● *Acknowledge the awkwardness.* All through the service we seek to be sensitive to those in the congregation who may feel awkward about what is happening. For instance, we raise our hands when we sing songs of praise; not everyone is used to that.

If even one person appears mystified, or on the verge of panic, I will wait for an appropriate juncture in the service and say something like, "Incidentally, this may the first time you've been in a place where there's open, expressive praise like this. I want to assure you that nothing weird is going to happen. Although, I can hear someone thinking right now, *What do you mean 'going to?' It already has!"*

They laugh, of course. But acknowledging that our service is different and some may feel awkward helps people relax.

• *Encourage partial participation.* Awkwardness about participating in our distinct worship practices can also be alleviated by encouraging partial participation. If the worship leader has invited people to raise their hands in song, yet senses some discomfort, he may say, "Raising hands may be new to you. That's okay. Instead, let's all just hold our hands out in front of us, palms up, like this, the way you would if you were going to say to someone, 'What would you like me to do for you?' In fact, as we do it, why don't we say that to the Lord: 'Lord, what would you have me do for you today?' "

Instead of making visitors do something completely unusual to them, and instead of isolating them in a sea of waving hands, this gets everybody to perform a modified, everyday act together. It also focuses people's attention away from the act and onto Christ.

• *Explain the service as it progresses.* The above example also shows another technique we use to make our visitors feel part of the service. From time to time we explain what we're doing: "The reason for special music is to help us focus not on the performers but on the Lord" or "This is why we raise our hands," or "This is why we sometimes applaud."

For example, I might say, "I'm reminded this morning of how the writer of the Book of Lamentations said, 'Let us lift up our hearts with our hands unto God in the heavens.' Have you ever felt like your heart has been stepped on? Have you ever felt your heart empty? Why don't we together take our hands and make them like a cup and say, 'Lord, here's my heart. I bring it to you. I need to be filled anew.' "

Naturally, we don't want to lecture about every part of the

service every Sunday, but we regularly try to integrate biblical teaching on what we do and why. Once newcomers understand the service better, they're more likely to participate.

Encourage Them to Interact

We encourage people to interact with one another during worship. This not only helps us be "in one accord," it also helps visitors experience warm, Christian fellowship. There are two major ways that happens in our services.

● *Greeting and affirming.* Interaction begins with the greeting. After the opening songs and invocation, I usually say something light, humorous, or happy. I may relate something that happened that week in the community or in my life. Sometimes it has a spiritual focus, sometimes not. But it's always bright and positive, and it's always tied to our greeting one another.

For example, one Easter Sunday I told the story of a pastor who was concerned about reports that the Christian education program was ineffective. He decided to check it out for himself. He stopped in a fourth-grade classroom and asked one of the students, "Janie, when is Easter and what happens on it?"

Janie said, "Well, Easter's in the fall, and we dress up in costumes and go trick-or-treating."

Oh, no! the pastor thought. *This really is a problem.* Hoping for better results, he tried another student. "Jimmy, can you tell me when Easter is and what happens on that day?"

Jimmy said, "Well, it's in the winter, and we put up the tree and decorate it and exchange gifts."

Now the pastor was queasy, so he went to Mikey, the smartest kid in the class. "When is Easter," he asked, "and what happens then?"

Mikey answered, "Well, Easter is in the springtime when Jesus came up from the grave."

"Very good!" the pastor said, relieved.

Then Mikey added, "And if he sees his shadow, he goes back, and we have six more weeks of winter."

When the laughter died down, I said, "As we greet each other this morning, turn to two or three people near you and say, "He didn't go back. He's alive and with us today!"

The place came alive as people turned to greet others around them. The introduction had helped create a warmer, less threatening atmosphere.

Sometimes we'll use a verse of Scripture or something from a song we've just sung to introduce the greeting. Whatever it is, we get the people to speak an affirmation to one another.

● *Sharing and praying.* The heart of the interaction in the service comes in what we call our ministry time. In the middle of the service, people form groups of three to five and share their requests, and then one person prays. We only spend about four minutes in the prayer circles, but we spend eight minutes or so leading into them with a song or a brief text — anything to sensitize us on how we need one another.

We emphasize four things during this time. First, one of the worship leaders mentions a specific need that each group will pray for. That way the entire congregation is focused on one concern together.

Second, each person is strongly encouraged to share one prayer request for himself or herself — not for a neighbor or distant relative. Such sharing helps us bear one another's burdens and function as a church.

Third, we underline that we're about to *pray.* This isn't group therapy or a psychological exercise, but an encounter with the living God.

Fourth, we expect the Holy Spirit to minister to us while we're praying. We encourage people to believe healing is available or that a word of comfort will come.

Since this act of worship may intimidate newcomers, as we move into that part of the service I'll say, "If you're visiting and this is new to you, please accept the invitation into the circle even if only to observe. It may be novel for you, but you're going to love it."

Even though these groups would seem threatening, I'm convinced they are one of the major reasons so many people become Christians in our service. Unbelievers are loved by people who believe Jesus is alive, and it impresses them.

Offer Opportunities for Commitment

Naturally, an unbeliever cannot fully engage in worship until he or she has made a commitment to Christ. Part of our service, then, is designed to encourage commitment. So, nine times out of ten, I will make an evangelistic appeal following the sermon.

"Every time we gather," I'll say, "there are some who have yet to begin their life with Jesus Christ. If you haven't begun trusting the Lord, you're aware of that. And there's nothing we can say or do that can force you to change. But we also know that when people come to our service, they often say, 'I feel the love of God in this place. I hear the ring of truth.'

"If that's you today, if you sense God's love and want to respond, then I invite you to open your heart to him."

This is not a time dripping with heaviness; it's not presented like a test they can fail. Instead, we simply give people an opportunity to respond.

A less traditional means we use to encourage commitment is the Lord's Supper. We invite all the people to gather around the Lord's Table and partake in small groups. We believe it is the Lord's Table we are invited to, the Lord is doing the inviting, and no one is excluded. To us that means unbelievers are invited, as well.

We explain clearly, of course, what we are doing, and what an unbeliever is doing by partaking: making a commitment to Christ. We stress the gravity of the event to reflect the serious nature of faith in Christ.

At the same time, we want people to know that they are welcome. For example, I might say, "If you are visiting with us today, you are not only welcome to participate, you are urged to. If you were at my house and it came dinner time, I wouldn't leave you sitting in the other room while I went to the dining room. And if you said, 'Well, I'm not really hungry,' I'd say, 'Come in and sit with us anyway.' Now, as we come to the Lord's Table, join us. And when the bread is served, take a portion."

After everyone is served, I continue, "Everyone here who knows the Lord Jesus might thank him for . . ." and here I'll encourage them to thank God for something that relates to the morning's teaching. "If you've never received Christ," I continue, "you might say, 'God, I know I can't earn salvation by partaking of this. But in receiving this, I'm telling you I'm opening myself to your life.' " If they are not ready to take that important step and partake of Communion, they are encouraged to sit with us at the table while we partake.

So the Lord's Supper is not only a significant time for the church body, we also use it as a way to incorporate non-Christians into the service, and some into the body.

We recognize using Communion as an evangelistic opportunity troubles many people, and for understandable reasons. We're not arguing that every church should do it, or that it is necessary for churches that want to include unbelievers in their services. But it is one of the ways we incorporate unbelievers into our service.

From Beginning to End: Sincerity

There is no part of our service, then, in which the non-Christian visitor is not invited to participate fully. But our goal is not mere participation. We want to nurture an atmosphere where people sense God's presence and respond to him.

We use all these means, then, not as mere techniques to get people to do what they don't want to do. For us they simply are ways to help the visitor experience the presence of God as we experience it. If we don't lead our service with a sincere yearning to know and love God, our service will become a mere manipulation of people's religious feelings.

By God's grace, we'll continue to maintain sincerity. After attending our service, dozens of people have said within my earshot, "I walked into this place, and from the time the people began singing, I began weeping." These are not emotionally troubled individuals, but strong, successful people who are impressed simply by the presence of God.

In the end, then, it is God, not anything we do, who draws people to himself. Our job as worship leaders is graciously to prepare the way.

No matter what is happening in the community, we gather to offer homage to the Most High God, and nothing should distract us from this purpose.
— *John Killinger*

CHAPTER TWELVE

Holydays and Holidays

On the Sunday nearest a recent Memorial Day, my wife and I attended a well-known church in Southern California. The church is noted for its pizzazz, but we hardly were prepared for everything that happened.

For starters, a Native American, dressed in buckskin jacket, sang "God Bless America," and the minister interviewed a recently returned Beirut hostage. Then a military squad paraded up and down the aisles, boots clicking smartly on the floor and rifles rotated and shouldered in striking precision.

Two high school bands came playing down the aisles, meeting before the chancel as majorettes twirled and spun their batons. As a finale, a dozen ushers marched across the chancel, carrying something that resembled an enormous carpet. When they had attached their burden to a series of wires, a ninety-foot American flag rose behind the choir, while the bands played, the majorettes twirled, the rifle guard stood at attention, and we all sang "The Battle Hymn of the Republic."

It was quite a show for the two dollars I dropped in the offering plate.

I went away thinking of Luther's phrase *the Babylonian captivity of the church* and wondering if perhaps he would have called this "the Hollywoodian captivity of the church."

But my misgivings about the appropriateness of this hooha placed me in a definite minority. Most of the congregants, I could tell from their whispers, were mightily impressed. Some even professed to have felt the presence of the Lord.

Our Puritan ancestors, of course, would have been apoplectic. They tended to disregard holidays and special events completely — even Christmas and Easter — and held to simple, unadorned worship of God. Psalms and prayers and admonitions were good enough for them Sunday after Sunday, with the admonitions often running to "twenty-seventhly" and "twenty-eighthly."

In our age, when special days for mothers, fathers, national independence, and the commemoration of notable historic figures and events is an integral part of community life, what *is* an appropriate liturgical approach?

A Convergence of Principles

Should Christians adhere strictly to their usual Sunday worship, or is it permissible to substitute, alter, or embellish our worship routines?

Two principles are involved.

The first is the principle of *integrity*. Worship is always, without exception, the worship of God. That fact is central. No matter whose birthday it is or what is happening in the community, we gather to offer homage to the Most High God. Nothing should distract us from this purpose.

Every service of worship, whether a regular Sunday service, a holiday service, a special anniversary service, or a service of installation for a new minister, should have as its singular purpose to set us once more in the presence of Almighty God. It is our opportunity for praise and prayer and for renewing faith and commitment. If our worship does not do this, then it is not worth our time and effort. We might as well join the great weekend migrations to the seashore or the Sunday pilgrimages to the ball park.

The second principle is *accommodation*. As we ponder the gospel, we see that God, in every age, has reached out to human beings. This is what the Incarnation was about — Deity enrobed in human flesh in order to reach us on our level, to speak in ways we could hear with our limited understanding.

Every worship service is imperfect, a fumbling attempt to frame praise, to recognize the Ineffable in our midst. It is, at best, a combination of words, sounds, and silences by which we try to focus our attention on the One who created and sustains our world. Granted, the Spirit inspires and directs our attempt, but we can never produce sounds and silences worthy of Almighty God.

Given that every worship service is in a sense an accommodation to human weakness, perhaps Christmas and Easter and Pentecost, and even Mother's Day, the Fourth of July, and Denominational Emphasis Day can be accommodated for worship. We are obligated, of course, to see that the principle of integrity is observed, so that all the hymns and prayers and innovative features point the worshiper unmistakably to God and not to a vacuum encased in frivolity. But considering who we are, and that our attention is more easily garnered by special decorations and emphases at certain times of the year, I believe our ability to worship, far from being hindered, is actually abetted by the observance of seasonal liturgies.

John Westerhoff and William Willimon even go so far as to say, in *Liturgy and Learning Through the Life Cycle*, that "without holidays our days will not become holy days." When we begin where people are, caught up in the spirit of special days and seasons, we can lead them more readily to an experience of the presence of God.

Following the Church Calendar

There is certainly nothing new in following the church calendar. As far back as Christians can recall, we've celebrated the days and seasons of the church year with "propers," prayers and readings traditionally attached to those days.

"Without the propers," says James F. White in *New Forms of Worship*, "Christian worship would become completely routine and monotonous. Awareness of the function of propers leads to a more lively presentation of the fullness of the gospel. Children, our best teachers about worship, have long demonstrated the importance of special occasions in communicating civic or historical meaning. A child lives from Halloween to Thanksgiving till Christmas, and so on throughout the year. And much of what he learns about America and Christianity is communicated by the yearly cycle. The Christian year provides one of our best means for adding interest and variety to worship."

A small step from using a variety of prayers and hymns is using other, more innovative means of altering our liturgies at particular times of the year. Families or other small groups giving Advent readings while lighting the candles of the Advent wreath, for example, add a meaningful dimension to worship. The readings can include both familiar passages and thoughtfully selected sentences or paragraphs from contemporary writings.

Suppose the Advent text "In those days John the Baptist came, preaching in the Desert of Judea and saying, 'Repent, for the kingdom of heaven is near' " (Matt. 3:1) were coupled with this reading from *Chop Wood, Carry Water*:

> [P. D.] Ouspensky [author of *In Search of the Miraculous*] met with his students when he knew he was dying. He refused to answer any of their questions about the system he had been teaching.

"Be simpler," he told them. "Start with what you know."

The necessary first step, then, is to acknowledge our present condition, even if it is (as it often is) one of confusion, hesitation, and doubt. This acknowledgement is the essence of spirituality. It is a simple act, but only by this simple act — seeing where we are rather than imagining where we would like to be — can we begin the process of transforming all those things we usually consider stumbling blocks into the stepping stones they really are.

Or consider linking "The people walking in darkness have seen a great light; on those living in the land of the shadow of death a light has dawned" (Isa. 9:2) with the description from Morris West's *The Clowns of God* of former Pope Gregory's experience of the mystical presence while recovering from a stroke:

Somewhere in the deep core of himself — that sorry fortress so beset and bombarded and ruined — there was a place of light where the Other dwelt, and where, when he could withdraw to it, there was communion of love, blissful but all too brief. It was like — what was it like? — deaf Beethoven with his head full of glories, Einstein bereft of mathematics to express the mysteries he understood at the end.

Many Protestants, realizing our ancestors sometimes threw out the meaning with the holy water, are now reclaiming Lent and Holy Week as times of worship and reflection. Lent is a wonderful time for a series of meditations/discussions/sermons on such topics as Disciplines of the Christian Life, In the Steps of the Master, Understanding the Mystics, and A Pilgrimage in Prayer. Studies such as these are designed to lead thoughtful Christians to a renewal of the inner life before the great celebration of Easter.

Having personally been involved in Ash Wednesday services from one end of the country to the other, I can testify to the excitement many Christians are finding in recovering this ancient liturgical occasion. When I've conducted such services, I've made clear to worshipers their option of not being marked by ashes (usually in the sign of the cross on the forehead) before proceeding to Communion, but few chose to abstain.

One prominent businessman said on such an occasion, "I don't think I've ever before fully understood the meaning of humility as I understand it now." He wore the smudge of ashes on his forehead all day and had many opportunities to witness to his faith among colleagues.

Holy Week Services

Palm Sunday gives us a marvelous day for reconsidering the values by which we live and the steadfastness or sincerity of the religious commitment we have made. In a service in which the children and choir members process with palm branches (easily obtainable from local florists), the congregation can voice the following prayer of confession:

> As our minds and hearts are drawn once more to the Holy City, O Lord, we realize how like our own city it was, filled with tension and intrigue, betrayal and violence. Forgive us for our shallowness and deceit, and for the willingness with which we would crucify Christ if he were here today. Help us look at ourselves and sob bitterly as Peter did, knowing that we are selfish and shortsighted, as he was. And grant that, having moved through the sad and somber events of this week, we shall be prepared for renewal and affirmation on Easter, when we celebrate your victory over evil and death. Amen.

Among our Holy Week observances at the First Congregational Church of Los Angeles were two unique services: one on Maundy Thursday evening and one on Easter eve.

The Maundy Thursday service began in the chapel with a call to worship, a hymn, a prayer, and an invitation to follow the deacons in a silent processional to the church's crypt. In the crypt, we took our places around candlelit tables arranged in the form of a cross. The deacons served a light meal of broth and brown bread, which we ate to the accompaniment of Scripture readings about the sufferings and crucifixion of Christ. A quartet sang hymns, and we celebrated Communion quietly.

After hearing more Scripture readings, ending with the words, "And they sang a hymn and went out," we sat in darkness as a light slowly illumined a large, wooden cross at the end of the room. A recording of "The Old Rugged Cross" sounded softly in the background. In unison, we arose and moved toward the cross, with each person pausing in silent prayer before passing through the doors.

The Easter eve service, designed many years ago by Dr. James W. Fifield, is called "The Service of the Holy Flame." It consists of a series of choral numbers and Scripture readings about the Crucifixion, alternately rendered, leading to a climax in the reading of Matthew 27:50–54, the passage about the earthquake at the time of the Crucifixion. While the passage is read, the organist improvises sounds of thunder and the splitting earth. The effect is dramatic, especially when the lights go out.

Then, as the words of the angel announcing the Resurrection are read, a great flame shoots up in the chancel (a special brazier, constructed years ago, is used for this), illuminating the front of the church. The Easter flowers, including a large cross of Easter lilies, previously draped in black cloth, become visible in their full glory. The choir bursts into the magnificent "Hallelujah" chorus, and the entire congregation stands in awe and respect.

Writing an invitation to the city of Los Angeles to attend this annual service, I once concluded, "Bring your own goosepimples!" I was being truthful. The service never failed to evoke such a response.

Easter was never anticlimactic. How could it be? But if such were ever possible, it would have been after these services during Holy Week.

The Coming of the Spirit

We place great emphasis on Christmas and the coming of God the Son, so therefore Pentecost, when we celebrate the coming of

God the Spirit, ought to command equal time. But often it doesn't. It is understandable, perhaps; a baby is easier to celebrate than a "holy ghost." But it leaves us in the wrong phase of the Christian story.

How do we convey the sense of thrill and discovery that marked that first Pentecostal experience?

One church I visited played a recording of a babble of voices over the amplifying system at intervals during the liturgy. Another broadcast a recording of the rushing wind. Another held a jazz service, with all the music played and sung in syncopated rhythm. Everybody — even the very old members — swayed and tapped their feet and clapped their hands in accompaniment. Everyone came out of church that day smiling and happy.

At our church in Los Angeles, we always concluded our Pentecost services in the church's forecourt, where the young people gave everyone a helium-filled balloon. At a given signal, we all released our balloons and watched them ascend like a colorful mosaic into the sky. Invariably, a gasp of delight went up from the crowd. People went away having heard — and seen — the promise of the gospel, that the divine Spirit is at work in the world, bringing all things to God's intended conclusion.

From Pentecost to Advent

The Christian year doesn't end with Pentecost and take up again with Advent. The season from one to the other is given over to the celebration of Christian mission in the world, and is replete with opportunities for special liturgies. The worship commission of the United Methodist Church decided a few years ago to rename this period Kingdomtide and to use it to reemphasize in a variety of ways the work of God's people under the leadership of the Spirit.

The season climaxes with All Saints' Day on November 1, the Christian version of Memorial Day, when we honor the memory of all the saints of God who have preceded us in the faith. The prior Sunday presents a grand occasion for emphasizing such themes as the perseverance of the saints, the priesthood of all believers, the communion of the saints, and the role of the saints in the work of the kingdom. It also can be a wonderful time for a service of dedication to recognize memorial gifts.

Churches with a strong sense of the Reformation tradition often combine the acknowledgement of All Saints with Reformation Day, October 31, which commemorates Martin Luther's tacking his Ninety-Five Theses to the door of the castle church in Wittenberg on October 31, 1517. The great Lutheran hymn "A Mighty Fortress" is heard in the same liturgy with Ralph Vaughan Williams's majestic rendering of "For All the Saints."

Along the way to Reformation Day and All Saints, many Protestant churches are beginning to join with Roman Catholics in celebrating the October birthday of Francis of Assisi, the founder of the Franciscan Order famed for his gentleness to animals. The theme for St. Francis' Day usually centers on world peace or respect for the entire created order of God.

A Host of Secular Occasions

Many pastors have no problem designing worship experiences for services covered by the church calendar, but they struggle with acknowledging such secular days as Mother's Day, Father's Day, Independence Day, and Labor Day. What should our position be?

Again I refer to the principles of integrity and accommodation. If the liturgies point unwaveringly to the glory of God, I don't hesitate to appropriate the interests and enthusiasms of the secular world and incorporate them into Christian worship.

Valentine's Day. This day, whose origin has at best a spurious relationship to Christian history, is a sensible time to talk about the true nature of love, distinguishing between the *eros* of popular tradition and the *agape* or undeserved love of the Christian gospel. It's not difficult to construct an entire liturgy around the subject of love. Here is a paraphrase of parts of 1 Corinthians 13 I wrote as a reading in such a liturgy:

> If I sing with the charisma of a rock star or speak with the power of Billy Graham, but haven't any love, I am as useless as a burglar alarm nobody pays any attention to. If I give

everything I have to feed the poor and house the homeless, and if I go to prison for the blacks of South Africa, and don't have any love, it isn't worth a single grain of rice!

Love bears the stress and truly cares about people. It doesn't worry when others get more than their due, and it isn't anxious to receive the credit. Love doesn't strut, full of its own glory. It doesn't deal rudely or abruptly with others. Love doesn't engage in gossip, or quietly enjoy when others get into trouble. Instead, it always looks for the good in people and situations.

Love possesses an almost inexhaustible capacity for belief and hope and endurance.

The ability to look into the future is all right, but it is limited. The same is true of the gift of tongues or the ability to know everything. The fact is, everything about us is human and therefore less than perfect, even our most heavenly talents and attributes.

Someday, when we are with the Lord, we will see everything aright. It all has to do with the seasons of our understanding. When we were preschoolers, we thought and behaved with the understanding of preschoolers. Now that we are grown, we see how much we knew or believed then was imperfect or ridiculous; and when we get to heaven, we will realize how much of what we know and understand now is also imperfect and ridiculous.

For now it is as though we look into a steamed-up mirror and can't see anything very clearly, but then the steam will be gone, and we will see everything as perfectly as if it were staring us in the face. Now, like the four blind men trying to describe an elephant, we understand only a small part of the truth; then, we shall be one with the truth, and everything we think and say will represent it fully and accurately.

Of all the meaningful things in life, having faith, being filled with hope, and experiencing love are among the most significant. But nothing compares with love. In this world, it is the greatest!

Mother's Day and Father's Day. These days of tribute offer similar opportunities to focus on the importance of love. For instance, here's a creed for the congregation to say on Mother's Day:

> I believe in Jesus Christ, the Son of the living God, who was born of the promise to a virgin named Mary.
>
> I believe in the love Mary gave her Son, that caused her to follow him in his ministry and stand by his Cross as he died.
>
> I believe in the love of all mothers, and its importance in the lives of the children they bear.
>
> It is stronger than steel, softer than down, and more resilient than a green sapling on the hillside.
>
> It closes wounds, melts disappointments, and enables the weakest child to stand tall and straight in the fields of adversity.
>
> I believe that this love, even at its best, is only the shadow love of God, a dark reflection of all that we can expect of Him, both in this life and the next.
>
> And I believe that one of the most beautiful sights in the world is a mother who lets this greater love flow through her to her child, blessing the world with the tenderness of her touch and the tears of her joy.
>
> Thank God for mothers, and thank mothers for helping us understand God!

The important thing, as demonstrated in this creed, is that all the materials of the liturgy — prayers, hymns, special music, unusual actions, and sermon — be compatible with the Christian faith and point the worshipers toward the God at the center of the faith.

Independence Day. This event, which can so easily become a trumpet-blowing, flag-waving occasion without reference to the Transcendent One, may be sensitively channeled into a worship experience that transforms our nationalism. Here, for example, is a prayer of confession for the congregation to use on the Sunday nearest the Fourth of July:

We confess to you, O Lord, our own sins and the sins of our nation: the sin of pride, when we have believed ourselves superior to others; the sin of despair, when we thought ourselves worse than others; the sin of greed, when we have sought our own welfare at the expense of others; the sin of wrongdoing, when we seized land or mistreated people without cause; the sin of poisoning the earth and sky and sea for our own selfish benefits; the sin of teaching our children to hate or to make war; the sin of pretending to be religious when we weren't. Send renewal in our time, O Lord; let the Spirit that was in Christ Jesus be now in us, that we may truly love you and that we may love our country for its great ideals and achievements, not for any sinful or selfish reasons. Amen.

I concluded this prayer with words of assurance using a citation from 2 Chronicles 7:14.

Leader: If my people, who are called by my name, will humble themselves,

People: If they will pray and seek my face,

Leader: If they will turn from their wicked ways,

People: Then I will hear from heaven and will forgive their sin and heal their land.

Leader: This is the word of the Lord. Amen.

Labor Day. This occasion, which to many means little except a welcome occasion for a three-day weekend, offers splendid opportunities for the church to relate its message to anyone who works.

One church in Texas arranged for thirty of its members to appear in the worship service on Labor Day Sunday wearing the work clothes of their various occupations. They lined up across the front of the chancel as the minister gave a brief sermon on the sanctity of work when done to glorify God.

Afterward, many congregants commented that the service had made them value their own work more highly, seeing its place in God's world. A woman who worked as a waitress told the minister weeks later, "Since that service, I've actually been proud of what I do, and every night as I am working, I thank God for my job."

Thanksgiving. The biggest secular holiday readily accepted by Christians is, of course, Thanksgiving Day, which belongs not just to the church but to the nation as a whole. Because it is entwined with the nation's history, it is a wonderful occasion for inviting whole segments of the community that do not usually worship with us, including our Jewish friends. Many Christians have found, in fact, that this is the holiday *par excellence* for communitywide services and have taken the lead in bringing together Jews, Roman Catholics, Greek Orthodox, and Protestant groups for the celebration of God's bounty to our country and its pluralistic population.

Not only have such services resulted in better friendships among the various groups involved, they also have also led to a cross-fertilization of liturgical traditions, with Jews understanding Christian feelings for the cross of Christ and Christians gaining new appreciation for the Torah-scroll borne into the service by the Jews.

The Joy of Worship

Dom Gregory Dix's *The Shape of the Liturgy*, first published more than fifty years ago, remains one of the seminal studies of worship. Its major thesis is that the hours and days of worship exist for the purpose of sanctifying all of time. When we turn aside from what we are doing at particular hours to wait before God in humility and love, we are, in effect, converting all our hours and days to his use and glory. The times of worship, like knots in a string, lend their character to the entire stretch of time, from the beginning to eternity.

If this is true, then worship, the sanctification of time, is the most important work we ever do. It should be the best we are capable of crafting and should represent our whole lives, not isolated segments of them.

When our worship is the best of which we are capable, we'll know the joy and satisfaction of helping ourselves and others worship God — a joy unmatched by the satisfaction of any other human undertaking.

Passion is an unstable element to add to worship. You never know where it will take a congregation. But worship without passion is like stacked wood without fire: orderly but cold and lifeless.

— *Mark Galli*

Epilogue

Apparently, the psalmists didn't care if worship was done decently and in order, or if things were left a bit messy afterwards. So they not only invited children to worship, but worse: "Praise the Lord . . . you sea monsters . . . beasts and all cattle, creeping things and flying birds!" I doubt Buildings and Grounds was pleased with that move.

Nor did the psalmists seem to care much about upsetting moribund deacons: "Praise him with trumpet sound; praise him with lute and harp! Praise him with timbrel and dance!"

Nor did they have much sympathy with those who argue that worship leaders should control their emotions: "I love thee, O Lord!" exclaimed one, and another shouted, "I will praise the Lord as long as I live; I will sing praises to my God while I have being!"

In short, they were extravagant, joyful, passionate people, these psalmists, who, if they were hired by a modern church, would take some getting used to. They'd want to hold on to history and tradition, all right — after all, they went on and on about the deliverance from Egypt — but they'd also keep looking for fresh ways to express praise. They weren't interested in newness for newness's sake; they simply wanted to engage the hearts of worshipers.

After reading these contributors to *Mastering Worship*, I'm convinced I've read some modern psalmists. Like those song-poets of old, they are driven by a deep love for God. They're also concerned about order and detail. Yet despite differences in theology and church culture, these three authors agree: worship requires not only thought, but a certain passion.

Passion, of course, is an unstable element to add to worship. You never know where it will take a congregation. But worship without passion is like stacked wood without fire: orderly but cold and lifeless.

So, it is for increasing passion in worship that we have offered this book. Naturally, passion will look different in Congregational, Foursquare, and Evangelical Free churches. But beneath different worship forms — the stacked wood of each tradition — a holy passion can light a fire that reveals to people the God of Mount Horeb and sends them forth in the power of Pentecost.

Bibliography:
Books Recommended
by the Authors

Collections of Prayers and Worship Aids

Baillie, John. *A Diary of Private Prayer*. New York: Scribner, 1978.

Barclay, William. *Prayers for the Christian Year*. Minneapolis: Augsburg Fortress.

Bennett, Arthur. *Valley of Vision*. Carlisle, Pa.: The Banner of Truth Trust, 1983.

Currie, David. *Come Let Us Worship God: A Handbook of Prayers for Leaders of Worship*. Louisville: Westminster, 1977.

Davies, Horton, and Morris Slifer. *Prayers and Other Resources for Public Worship*. Nashville: Abingdon, 1976.

Killinger, John. *Lost in Wonder, Love, and Praise: Prayers and Affirmations for Christian Worship*. Lynchburg, Va.: Angel Books (P.O. Box 3390, Lynchburg, Virginia 24503), 1986.

Miller, Samuel H. *Prayers for Daily Use*. New York: Harper and Brothers Publishers, 1957.

Phillips, E. Lee. *Prayers for Worship*. Grand Rapids: Baker, 1985.

Savage, Robert. *Pocket Praise*. Wheaton: Tyndale, 1985.

Thorne, Leo S. *Prayers from Riverside*. New York: Pilgrim, 1983.

Zurdel, Veronica, ed. *Eerdman's Book of Famous Prayers*. Grand Rapids: Eerdmans, 1984.

Hymn Helps

Bock, Fred and Bryan J. Leech. *The Hymnal Companion*. Nashville: Paragon-Benson, 1979.

Osbeck, Kenneth. *One Hundred and One Hymn Stories*. Grand Rapids: Kregel, 1982.

Osbeck, Kenneth. *One Hundred and One More Hymn Stories*. Grand Rapids: Kregal, 1985.

Sullivan, Francis Patrick. *Lyric Psalms: Half a Psalter*. Washington, D.C.: The Pastoral Press, 1983.

Literature Conducive to Use in Worship

Alexander, Pat, ed. *Eerdmans' Book of Christian Poetry*. Grand Rapids: Eerdmans, 1981.

Brandt, Leslie. *Epistles Now*. St. Louis: Concordia, 1976.

Brandt, Leslie. *Jesus Now*. St. Louis: Concordia, 1978.

Brandt, Leslie. *Prophets Now*. St. Louis: Concordia, 1979.

Brandt, Leslie. *Psalms Now*. St. Louis: Concordia, 1973.

Fields, Rick. *Chop Wood, Carry Water: A Guide to Finding Spiritual Fulfillment in Everyday Life*. Los Angeles: Jeremy P. Tarcher, Inc., 1984.

History and Theology of Worship

Allen, Ronald, and Gordon Borror. *Worship: Rediscovering the Missing Jewel*. Portland, Oreg.: Multnomah, 1987.

Brown, Robert McAfee. *Spirituality and Liberation*. Philadelphia: Westminster, 1988.

Dix, Dom Gregory. *The Shape of the Liturgy*. New York: Harper & Row, 1982.

Hayford, Jack. *Worship His Majesty*. Irving, Tex.: Word, 1987.

Ortland, Anne. *Up with Worship*. Ventura, Cal.: Regal, 1982.

Thompson, Brad, ed. *Liturgies of the Western Church*. Minneapolis: Augsburg Fortress, 1980.

Webber, Robert. *Celebrating Our Faith: Evangelism Through Worship.* New York: Harper & Row, 1986.

Westerhoff, John, and William Willimon. *Liturgy and Learning Through the Life Cycle.* New York: Seabury, 1980.

White, James F. *New Forms of Worship.* Nashville: Abingdon Press, 1971.